THE REMINISCENCES OF

Captain Grayson Merrill
U.S. Navy (Retired)

INTERVIEWED BY

Paul Stillwell

U.S. Naval Institute • Annapolis, Maryland

Copyright © 1997

Preface

This oral history came about as the result of an article in the Annapolis newspaper last year. The article featured a picture of Captain Merrill at his home near Annapolis and reported a signal honor that would soon be coming his way. In October 1996 the Naval Air Warfare Center Weapons Division at Point Mugu, California, would be celebrating its 50th anniversary. To mark the event three buildings would be named in honor of individuals who made significant contributions to the command at Point Mugu. The center's Missile Dystems Evaluation Laboratory would be named for Captain Merrill, an officer who has been unofficially recognized as the "founding father of Point Mugu."

The newspaper article concluded with a quotation from Captain Merrill: "One of the things I'm appreciating later in life is the importance of history. It's an educational thing and a motivational thing. If some young guys see what we old buzzards have done, maybe they'll say, 'Well, we can do that, too.'" Given that philosophy, Captain Merrill was most agreeable when an invitation to do an oral history resulted from the article. The interviews began shortly after his participation in the building naming and other 50th-anniversary activities. The following memoir chronicles a number of achievements during the period when guided missiles were in their infancy in the U.S. Navy.

Up to a point, Grayson Merrill had the standard career path for a line officer of his generation. He graduated from the Naval Academy in 1934, had junior officer duties in surface ships, took flight training at Pensacola, and then served in fleet aviation squadrons. At the outset of World War II, he set out on a much different course than the traditional. Pulled out of postgraduate school with the advent of World War II, he spent much of the wartime period involved with the development of pilotless aircraft, including assault drones and early guided missiles. Captain Merrill provides a great many insights on the late Rear Admiral Del Fahrney, who was his mentor and another guided missile pioneer.

Captain Merrill recommended that the Navy get into the missile business following World War II, and he helped import German rocket scientists to facilitate the process. He recommended the establishment of a missile test center and was on the selection committee that led to the choice of Point Mugu as the site for the Navy's missile testing range in the Pacific. He was on hand when Point Mugu was commissioned in 1946 and had much to do with laying the groundwork for its long-term success. Included was a three-year stint as director of tests. In the mid-1950s he was the first technical director for the Polaris program that developed a deterrent force of submarine-launched ballistic missiles. He is candidly critical in assessing the leadership and management of Rear Admiral William "Red" Raborn, who ran the Special Projects Office that brought Polaris into being.

In the course of moving from the initial raw transcript of the oral interviews to this final version, both Captain Merrill and I have done considerable editing in the interests of accuracy, smoothness, and clarity. In addition, Captain Merrill worked over the transcript on his personal computer and added some written sections to supplement the transcript of the oral interviews. I have added footnotes to provide additional information for readers who use the volume. Ms. Ann Hassinger of the Naval Institute's history division has made a significant contribution through her diligence in the overall process of printing, proofreading, and overseeing the binding of the completed volumes.

Paul Stillwell
Director, History Division
U.S. Naval Institute
October 1997

CAPTAIN GRAYSON MERRILL
UNITED STATES NAVY (RETIRED)

Grayson Merrill was born New Year's Day 1912 in Los Angeles, California. He enlisted in the Navy in 1929, received recruit training in San Diego, and attended a preparatory school there prior to being appointed to the Naval Academy in 1930. Following his graduation and commissioning as an ensign in 1934, he served for a year in the battleship West Virginia (BB-48). He then had brief tours of duty in the destroyers Brooks (DD-232) and Dorsey (DD-117) in the Pacific prior to reporting in 1936 for Navy flight training at Pensacola, Florida. After receiving his wings as a naval aviator the following year, he served in Torpedo Squadron Three, based on board the aircraft carrier Saratoga (CV-3). Subsequently he had a tour of duty as a pilot in Utility Squadron One.

In mid-1941, Merrill began to take an abbreviated electrical engineering course at the Naval Postgraduate School, Annapolis, Maryland. His education was short-lived, because in early 1942 Commander Delmar S. Fahrney selected him to be his deputy in the Special Design Branch of the Bureau of Aeronautics, where the Navy's first guided missiles were being developed. As a team, these two officers then formulated and directed much of the navy's World War II and early postwar guided missile efforts.

In 1943 Fahrney was reassigned as head of the Naval Air Modification Unit at the Naval Aircraft Factory, Philadelphia, and Merrill succeeded him as head of the Special Design Branch. Merrill then faced the task of supporting the engineering and production program for the assault drone program. He also directed the continuing development of the glided bomb and the series of Gorgon missiles begun under Captain Fahrney. Thereafter, Merrill initiated and directed the development of the following weapons in response to wartime requirements: the Lark surface-to-air missile; the Gargoyle air-to-surface missile, and the Little Joe ship-to-air missile. The latter was a quick-fix response to the devastating attacks then being made by the Japanese kamikaze suicide bombers.

Within a year after taking over from Fahrney, Merrill became convinced of the necessity for an instrumented Navy missile sea test range. Although there were limited test facilities at the Special Weapons Tactical Test and Evaluation Unit (SWTTEU) at Traverse City, Michigan, the Navy still had to test the longer-range missiles from various East Coast naval air stations over heavily used shipping lanes. It was against this background in October 1944 that Merrill drafted a letter detailing the requirements and recommendations for a missile sea test range, which the Chief of the Bureau of Aeronautics signed out to the Chief of Naval Operations. In his letter Commander Merrill presented a case of urgent need for an over-water range as vital to the development of the growing field of naval missile weaponry. He also asked for the establishment of a board of officials to survey and evaluate possible sites for such a range.

Following the CNO's concurrent with Merrill's recommendations, a site survey board was established in January 1945 to investigate the potential locations for the Naval Air Special Missiles Test Center, later renamed the Naval Air Missile Test Center. The board was headed by Captain W. V. Vieweg and supported by ten other members, including Commander Merrill. The board investigated 26 sites on the East, West, and Gulf coasts, as well as the Caribbean area.

At Point Mugu, California, the board found a large waterfront area already under lease from private owners by the Navy's Construction Battalion Center at Port Hueneme.

There were some Quonset huts, a few wooden barracks, and a 3,000-foot Marston aircraft landing mat laid down by Seabee training classes. The nearby 1,500-foot Laguna Peak and the outlying chain of Channel islands, along with the Navy-owned San Nicholas Island, offered the potential for multiple locations for tracking, receiving, and surveillance stations. The coastal shipping lanes were judged as not being a major problem, and the presence of a nearby Navy-operated deep-sea port at Port Hueneme was seen as a desirable factor.

The board's final recommendation to CNO, drafted by Commander Merrill in March 1945, was that Point Mugu was by far the most suitable of all sites investigated and that the test center should be located there. The draft also contained a proposed layout and plan for the development of the center and the prediction by Merrill that "this site will meet the Navy's needs twenty-five years hence." The proposal was approved by the entire chain of command.

In late 1945 Merrill left the Bureau of Aeronautics to become the new center's technical director (a title soon changed to director of tests) of the Naval Air Missile Test Center, then being staged at the Mojave Naval Air Station prior to being moved to Point Mugu. At Mojave during the winter of 1945-46 he worked with Commander Ernest Christensen, former SWTTEU commander, to develop preliminary facility requirements and the first organizational structure for the new center. At the same time he was overseeing test operations of the Lark, Gorgon, and Gargoyle missiles and KD2R-2, KDH-1, and KD3H-1 target drones.

As director of tests at the Naval Air Missile Test Center for three years, Commander Merrill was responsible for all facets of the developing center except the administrative ones. He worked with the officer in charge of construction to plan all the buildings and facilities; he oversaw development of the technical organization, instrumentation of the range, design of test procedures, and approved the hiring of all key civilians.

During the late summer of 1945 Commander Merrill learned about a large group of German scientists who had agreed to be brought to the United States under "Project Paper Clip" to work on weapons programs. He visited them at the Naval Special Devices Center at Port Washington, New York, where they had been sequestered. After talking with several of them, he became convinced that they would be highly useful at Point Mugu once it was established. He placed a request for 12 of them, including Dr. Herbert Wagner, designer of the HS-293 flying bomb that the German Luftwaffe first used in combat in 1943.

The selected scientists arrived at Point Mugu over the period of 1947-48. Merrill chose a different approach for using them than did the Army, which permitted Wernher von Braun to keep his group together as a team. Instead, Merrill chose to use his transplanted talent to supplement the technical capabilities of his new work force. He did this by assigning them to individual projects or laboratories akin to their proven specialities, where they could work directly with civilian counterparts. This approach proved productive in both the direct knowledge imparted by the Germans to the rest of the technical work force, as well as to the many new or improved designs they developed in optical and radar instrumentation, launching devices, airframes and guidance systems. One of them, Robert Lusser, developed and published the mathematical theory for determining missile reliability, while Dr. Wagner worked with the Marines to develop an all-weather close-air-support guidance system.

Commander Merrill left the Naval Air Missile Test Center for the Bureau of Aeronautics in mid-1949, at the same time Captain Fahrney was arriving to serve as commander of the center. At the bureau Merrill had a brief assignment in the guided missile division before being transferred to the Naval Air Development Center at Johnsville, Pennsylvania. Here he was once again engaged in missile design and development. During his final tour of active duty, prior to retirement from the Navy in 1957, Captain Merrill was the first technical director for the Polaris submarine-launched ballistic missile program.

In his post-Navy civilian employment he was chief engineer of Fairchild Aviation's Guided Missile Division and later president of PRD Electronics, a division of the Harris Corporation.

Between 1950 and 1960 Captain Merrill coauthored and edited a 13-volume series of university-level textbooks titled "Principles of Guided Missile Design," published by D. Van Nostrand. For this effort, the American Rocket Society gave him the G. Edward Pendray Award for excellence in technical literature. The purpose of these volumes was to disseminated missile technologies developed by the services during the war and thereby help defense contractors, designers, and engineers prepare for the postwar expansion in missile weaponry.

Authorization

The U.S. Naval Institute is hereby authorized to make available to individuals, libraries, and other repositories of its choosing the transcripts of three oral history interviews concerning the life and naval career of the undersigned. The interviews were recorded on 25 October 1996, 7 November 1996, and 17 January 1997 in collaboration with Paul Stillwell for the U.S. Naval Institute.

The undersigned does hereby release and assign to the U.S. Naval Institute the rights and title to these interviews, with the exception that the undersigned retains the right to use the material for his own purposes, as he sees fit. The copyright in both the oral and transcribed versions shall be the sole property of the U.S. Naval Institute. The tape recordings of the interviews are and will remain the property of the U.S. Naval Institute.

Signed and sealed this __3RD__ day of __MARCH__ 1997.

_____
Captain Grayson Merrill, USN (Ret.)

Interview Number 1 with Captain Grayson Merrill, U.S. Navy (Retired)

Place: Captain Merrill's home, Annapolis, Maryland

Date: Friday, 25 October 1996

Interviewer: Paul Stillwell

Q: Captain, I'm delighted that we're having a chance to get started here, after our previous meeting, to begin to cover your life. Could you please start at the beginning, telling me when and where you were born and something about your family?

Captain Merrill: Okay. I was born in Los Angeles, California, in 1912--on the first of January, incidentally--and was raised in California. My grandfather was a developer, one of the early developers in Los Angeles. We lived in a home on top of Mount Washington, which is just above the county courthouse. At any rate, I can barely remember my first four years there. At the fourth year, my father died of appendicitis while on a trip. And that, of course, changed the whole life-style of my family.

At that time I had one sister, Eunice, three years younger than I, and my mother was obliged to work in a hamburger stand down in Los Angeles to try to support her family. Fortunately, the Masons of California learned of her situation, and I eventually entered the Masonic Home together with my sister. It's a semi-orphan home in Covina, California. That would be when I was about ten, I guess. We were raised there, going to public schools--Covina High School, in my case.

I became oriented toward the Naval Academy when I was forced to think ahead by the superintendent of the Masonic Home, John Downen. It was a sort of a last resort; it was the only thing I could come up with at the moment.

Q: How good a student had you been in the years coming along?

Captain Merrill: I was quite a good student. In a class of perhaps 50, I was about number two. I worked pretty hard because it was a disciplined school and a disciplined home. I felt loved and cared for there very much. The people wanted me to succeed, and I knew it; I responded to that. So I set that goal for myself, about halfway through high school.

Q: I suspect that going to that home made an enormous difference in your life, compared with what would have happened had you continued to live with your mother.

Captain Merrill: Yes, it certainly did. And, as I say, I have great respect for the Masonic Home and others like it.

Q: Do you have any memories of your father?

Captain Merrill: Just barely. I can remember that he supervised my cruising around an empty tennis court in a stroller, and things of that nature. He had a good voice, and at that particular time his father was fairly well off. He sent Dad and his wife, before the children came along, to New York to study voice for several months. I remember him coming back and singing. But, of course, beyond his death, I have no memories.

Q: What sort of work did he do?

Captain Merrill: He helped his father in the real estate developing business.

Q: Was that essentially a boom period in California real estate?

Captain Merrill: Well, it was when he started it, which was 1912 or thereabouts. But it quickly took a turn for the worse. I think the economic situation deteriorated about 1916.

Q: We all know of the present hubbub and congestion and so forth around Los Angeles. What do you remember of the atmosphere there at the time?

Captain Merrill: First, the physical atmosphere was clean. I can remember looking up many nights and clearly seeing stars. Remember, this is was in the heart of downtown Los Angeles; today it is the center of the city's smog. But the degeneration of the city is probably what you're referring to.

Q: Right.

Captain Merrill: Culturally and environmentally it has gone steadily downhill. It was a middle-class, pretty much all-white community at that point in time. It suffered the same expansion problems that many other towns and cities did: New York, Washington, and so forth.

Q: What subjects were you particularly good at in school?

Captain Merrill: I was probably best in mathematics and science. I was not too good in English, but I caught up later on and became quite literate in writing and conversational English.

Q: With this Masonic influence, how much religion was there in your early life?

Captain Merrill: Not very much, but I would like to mention that my mother's father, my grandfather Hatch, was a Presbyterian minister, and I did live in his home for about a year. I suppose I was then around eight, and I can remember attending church regularly because of his status. I can also remember that when I dozed off in the congregation, he had a small wooden mallet with which he whacked the pulpit to wake me up. I still have the mallet somewhere.

Q: [Laughter] Did you have an inclination toward sports in those years?

Captain Merrill: Yes, quite a bit. In high school I played "lightweight" football, was on the track team and so forth, even though I probably weighed about 115 pounds. So I had a fairly active athletic program going.

Q: What sorts of hobbies did you have?

Captain Merrill: All inexpensive! It was a fairly austere environment, and the lack of money forced us to be innovative. One hobby that I can remember emerged from the fact that the Masonic Home was located on a farm. The farm had some orange trees, and it also had a stock of animals. I can remember horses and hogs; I became quite fond of the hogs. They were friendly. So I was commissioned to take the garbage from the dining room, which was perhaps 1,000 feet away, down to the hog pens and feed them. At one point, when it became evident that I would probably go to the Naval Academy, I learned that I had to arrive there with at least $100.00, because they wanted to be sure that they had enough money to send me back to California if I flunked out. So the way I got the $100.00 was by breeding and selling these hogs. That worked out just fine.

Q: Was doing chores at the farm understood as part of the whole arrangement with the home?

Captain Merrill: Yes, definitely. We were required to do spelled-out chores--outside of school hours, of course. And there was no nonsense about it; we did them, albeit with little enthusiasm.

Q: How much of an influence was your mother in your life after you had moved to the home?

Captain Merrill: I would see her about once a week. She worked in a department store, in charge of the art department. She had a gentleman friend but never married again. This friend would drive her out, in a Model-T Ford, from Los Angeles to Covina. I remember having many visits with her there. So, even though we were out of touch, we had those visits. Later on, when I went to the Naval Academy, we wrote frequently back and forth. So I didn't lose touch with her.

Q: And it sounds as if there was enough contact to sustain the emotional bond.

Captain Merrill: Yes, definitely.

Q: What was the process by which you got to the Naval Academy?

Captain Merrill: Unbeknownst to me, the superintendent of the home had made arrangements with a leading Mason who had contacts with Senator Shortridge of California; he received an appointment semi-commitment from the senator.[*] At this point I was a junior in high school. As time went on, I never knew this was going on, because they didn't want me to be disappointed.

In the meantime, I was looking into things on my own hook. I made a trip on the "Big Red" electric car that went between Covina and Los Angeles and there visited the naval recruiting station. There I got convinced by the recruiter that the thing to do was enlist in the Navy and try for an appointment. The Navy had 100 fleet appointments at that time. That was what I decided to do. So I enlisted in June of 1929. They put me into a sort of black paddy wagon, along with several other youngsters, and drove us down to San Diego. There I went through boot camp, probably the most educational experience of my life.

Q: How rigorous was the screening process for people getting into the Navy in those years?

---

[*] Samuel M. Shortridge (Republican-California) served in the U.S. Senate from 1921 to 1933.

Captain Merrill: Well, they weren't demanding. For example, they were not demanding a high school graduation. I would say that they were looking for teenagers that were more or less dependable, for example, from an environment in which they were comfortable and therefore not liable to desert. They were looking less for education and athletic background than they were stability, good health, and character.

Q: Well, of course, later in the '30s, because of the Depression, the Navy could afford to be very selective because so many people were available.[*]

Captain Merrill: Exactly. This was in June of '29, before the stock market crash. So they had to work at getting people to enlist.

Q: How much awareness did you have during this period of the wider world: Lindbergh's flight, overseas developments, and what have you?[†]

Captain Merrill: I think I was about as well informed as any average boy of that age. We had newspapers to look at. The radio (AM only) was just coming in, and we had one crystal set at the home. We would gather around it and take turns listening with the headset. So I suppose for that time, we were in touch with the world.

Q: Did you enjoy reading, per se?

Captain Merrill: I can't say I was an avid reader, no. I was more oriented toward the outdoors: hiking in the hills and athletic programs. Most of my reading was aimed at keeping up my academics in school. I was very focused in that department.

---

[*] Following the crash of the New York Stock Exchange in late October 1929, the United States was plunged into the Great Depression, from which it did not recover until the nation geared up for World War II at the beginning of the 1940s. The Depression was marked by high unemployment and many business failures.

[†] Charles A. Lindbergh became a national hero when he made the first solo flight across the Atlantic Ocean in May 1927. The light cruiser Memphis (CL-13) brought Lindbergh and his plane back to the United States, arriving at the Washington Navy Yard on 11 June.

Q: Did you have role models at the home and school that pushed you forward?

Captain Merrill: To some degree, yes. I mentioned the superintendent, John Downen, who was a man of integrity and high values. I felt he wanted to do his job and do it well. He was interested enough in each of us to take us aside now and then and talk about things. Looking back, I think that his was a wonderful institution, that Masonic Home. I visited it perhaps eight years ago, and it looks just as good as ever. They had completely new buildings, but the spirit was still there. I sensed the same relationship between the staff and the children.

Q: Remarkable to have that longevity.

Captain Merrill: Yes, it's still there; changed a lot, of course, but functionally it's the same.

Q: Did any part of your inspiration to go into the Navy result from being in the main fleet base during those years, Los Angeles Harbor, San Pedro?

Captain Merrill: I don't think so. You know, I wasn't that well informed about the Navy. I had no Navy role models in my family, nor was I in contact with such. It was just an opportunity for me at that point.

Q: How did you first become aware of that opportunity?

Captain Merrill: I don't remember. Mr. Downen sat me down in the baseball bleachers one afternoon and asked where I wanted to go to college. The word "Annapolis" popped out, and that became a focus for me. Later I went down to the recruiting station to find out more.

Q: After you got into the paddy wagon, what experiences did you have then?

Captain Merrill: All of us are familiar with various boot camp movies; clearly they're exaggerated. I can remember a chief petty officer named Allendorff. I'm sure he's long since gone. He was a little, wiry fellow who took us all in hand because he was responsible for our company. Each company had about 100 men, I guess. Under Allendorff's supervision, each man drew a seabag full of Navy uniforms, toilet articles, etc. By the way, I came down there with nothing. I think perhaps I had $5.00 in my pocket, and that was about it. But I did have $100.00 stashed away in the bank. Those were my assets. Again, it was an experience that I still admire. Allendorff was alternately a surrogate mother or a tough-minded father.

Q: Was this at San Diego?

Captain Merrill: San Diego, right. They took us all in, treated us reasonably well, bawled us out when we warranted it, and disciplined us when we erred. It was probably one of the best experiences of my life. It straightened me out as to any lackadaisical attitudes I had.

Q: Had the Masonic Home prepared you for the regimentation of boot camp?

Captain Merrill: To quite a degree, yes.

Q: What specific experiences do you remember from boot camp?

Captain Merrill: We were all housed in a barracks, each slept in a canvas hammock some two feet next to its neighbors. These hammocks were strung between horizontal, parallel pipes. One of the characters next to me was from Texas. He was a bully type, and I was pretty small compared to him. So he started working on me. On the other hand, there was another even larger boy who was more to my liking. He took up my cause, straightening out the guy from Texas by physical activity, if you know what I mean.

Q: I can make a deduction, yes.

Captain Merrill: [Laughter] So those kinds of things went on, and the pecking order was established.

Soon after boot camp it became evident that they were going to put me into the Naval Academy Prep School down there. That was a very unusual thing. Probably they had looked into my record after another thing had happened. Senator Shortridge had called the home and said he was ready to appoint this fellow Merrill. So the superintendent called me from Covina and said, "What do you want to do now?"

I replied, "Well, let's accept the appointment. I'm scheduled to go to the prep school, but I know I can pass the examination; there's no problem there." So that's what happened. I was finally appointed by Senator Shortridge, even though I was in the boot camp at that point. That worked out fine.

Q: So did you then avoid the prep school completely?

Captain Merrill: No, I went through with that.

Q: Oh, I see.

Captain Merrill: I went through that, because the time scale was such that I couldn't get into the academy in June of 1929. There was already a class entering. So I entered the Naval Academy in the summer of 1930 after a year in the Naval Academy Prep School.

Q: Was it geared to the Naval Academy entrance exams?

Captain Merrill: Exactly, focused entirely on that.

Q: What do you recall of the method of teaching and the curriculum?

Captain Merrill: Well, it was by rote. You studied mathematics, you solved problems. You advanced from one type of mathematics to another or chemistry or whatever it was. There were naval officers teaching; some of them were good, and some were pretty bad--I mean, in the sense that they didn't know their subjects very well and they weren't trained as teachers, but it all worked out. I think, in general, that their success rate in having their students pass the exam was excellent, considering that the students came from fairly low economic levels as to class of family.

Q: And probably lesser education than you had.

Captain Merrill: Right. But they did very well. I would guess that perhaps 85% of them passed the exam and got in.

Q: That's impressive.

Captain Merrill: It is.

Q: Where was the prep school geographically?

Captain Merrill: It was right at the Naval Training Station.

Q: Did some of your classmates in there consist of people who had come in from the fleet?

Captain Merrill: I would guess it was about 50%. Some of them, by the way, became very good friends of mine and went through the Naval Academy and beyond.

Q: Do you think that was a useful year to have under your belt before you took the exams?

Captain Merrill: Yes. It was very formative as to coping with real life.

Q: It probably lessened the culture shock when you got to Annapolis.

Captain Merrill: Yes, I would say so.

Q: Did you have any problems on the physical exams?

Captain Merrill: The only problem that turned up was when I actually got to the Naval Academy, and some doctor gave me a cursory examination and thought he heard a heart murmur. That led to a second examination, and another doctor cleared me.

Q: Well, here we are quite a few years later, and you've obviously survived.

Captain Merrill: Yes. It was a great life. I enjoyed it. There were moments of discomfort, let's say, but . . .

Q: We all have those.

Captain Merrill: Sure.

Q: What are your first memories of Annapolis and entering the Naval Academy?

Captain Merrill: Here's one memory. When I was in the prep class, in the middle of the academic year, which would be the winter, I took the exam for the Naval Academy. Now, the rest of them took it for practice, but I took it for the record, and I passed it. So the Navy very kindly said, "Well, what do you want to do with the six months between now and when you go back to the Naval Academy?"

I said, "Well, I wouldn't mind going on leave." So I did.

Q: For six months.

Captain Merrill: Yes. I used that up mostly at the home and being with my family. Then I elected to take a commercial steamship back to Baltimore; it was called the <u>Virginia</u>. Of course, the Navy paid for the travel. The ship went through the Panama Canal. I had a great time there, because I was in seaman second class uniform. I had started as an apprentice seaman, the lowest rank in the Navy. Today I'm very proud of that. Anyway, as a second class seaman on this vessel, the captain decided that I should stand some watches up on the bridge. He asked me to do it, and I was only too glad to do so. So I found myself up there taking bearings, steering, etc., all the way to Baltimore.

Q: Great indoctrination too.

Captain Merrill: Right. When I got up to Baltimore, I tried to find out how best to get down to Annapolis. It turned out that there was an electric streetcar line from Baltimore to Annapolis called the WB&A. Later I learned the letters stood for Wobble, Bounce, and Amble. [Laughter] So I got on this WB&A with my seabag full of uniforms, etc., and came down in a car going through places that I never dreamed I'd be living right next to.

When I got down here, I was pretty exhausted, and I went to a motel, because it was late at night. I fell asleep, and the desk clerk failed to wake me up, so I was late reporting into the Naval Academy.

Q: Would this be now June of 1930?

Captain Merrill: June of 1930, right. I got bawled out immediately for being late, but I survived. Then I went into plebe year and, of course, it's the standard story from there on in.[*]

Q: Well, please tell me what that standard story consisted of in your case.

---

[*] A midshipman in his first year is called a plebe; second year, youngster or third classman; third year, second classman; fourth year, first classman.

Captain Merrill: Okay. Most of the story, of course, involves your progress through the academic year. And I did quite well, I "starred," as they say, during my plebe year. You put a gold star on each side of your collar. I was in the upper 10% of the class and quite proud of that. I also found out that my physical size effectively barred me from any sports achievements. I went out for track and tried wrestling, but my athletic record was not impressive. My "aptitude for the service" was also low.

Q: What experiences do you remember from plebe summer and that socialization?

Captain Merrill: One of the things that I remember is the efforts that the families in Annapolis made to be hosts at tea parties, which we used to call "tea fights." In these parties we met some of the local girls, plus a fair number of imports from nearby girls' schools. That helped a great deal. Of course, I didn't have any family here. I kept in touch with them, but I developed some friendships in the community. That was about all the socialization that I can recall. The rest of it was just work, except for going to football games and getting excited about Army-Navy rivalry.

Q: What do you remember about the atmosphere in Bancroft Hall?*

Captain Merrill: It was pleasant. The focus was just to get up one day, attend classes, get your homework done, and get enough sleep to cope with the next day. There wasn't much time to get into mischief, although some of my classmates managed to be proficient at it.

Q: Please, do tell.

Captain Merrill: Well, of course, there were many who went "over the wall," as we called it. There was a wall, and still is, which confined midshipmen to the Naval Academy

---

* Bancroft Hall is the large multi-wing dormitory that houses Naval Academy midshipmen. It also contains the offices of members of the executive department, including the commandant, executive officer, and battalion and company officers.

grounds in no uncertain terms, especially in the plebe and youngster years. But the more adventurous mids--not me--went over the wall. Some got "papped" and punished in the way of drills or served time in the brig on the prison ship Reina Mercedes.* No serious crimes, that I know of--certainly none like what we read about today.†

Q: More mischievous, I take it.

Captain Merrill: It was more mischievous, yes, usually not involving sexual harassment. I don't think we even had that term.

Q: I'm confident you didn't.

Captain Merrill: [Laughter] It was a great life.

Q: What do you remember about the camaraderie with your classmates?

Captain Merrill: It was great. It has become better since we all graduated. As a matter of fact, yesterday I was at a class luncheon, which I enjoyed very much.

Q: Well, before we started the tape you mentioned Roy Smith, and he was an exception in that he didn't graduate.‡

---

* USS Reina Mercedes (IX-25), captured during the Spanish-American War, served as a station ship at the Naval Academy from 1912 to 1957. Until 1940, midshipmen being punished for various disciplinary infractions slept and took meals on board the ship but continued to go to classes ashore.
† During the mid-1990s the news media reported a number of criminal activities on the part of Naval Academy midshipmen. Included were murder, car theft, breaking and entering, and child molestation.
‡ Captain Roy C. Smith III, USNR (Ret.), entered the Naval Academy with the class of 1934 but left in December 1933 for disciplinary infractions described in his mother's Naval Institute oral history. He completed his degree at a civilian university.

Captain Merrill: That's right. I can't remember just why. Now, wait a minute. What happened to him?

Q: Well, he got caught coming back after he had Frenched out.*

Captain Merrill: Well, he's one of the characters I'm talking about, and I didn't even remember that or know about it. Well, it just goes to show you that a little mischief might be beneficial. Mean stuff, I don't countenance; I don't like that.

Q: Well, I think some people took satisfaction from trying to beat the system.

Captain Merrill: They did; they sure enough did.

Q: Do you remember examples of that, other than going over the wall?

Captain Merrill: Well, I remember one example that I was talking to Roy about yesterday. We had a fellow in our class--still alive and kicking--whose nickname was Screwy Lew, and then we had his great and good friend Peyton Magruder.†

At any rate, we were on the Arkansas, at anchor in Funchal Harbor, Madeira, when these two hatched up a plot.‡ One of them would leap over the side at night when everybody was watching a movie, and then the other would cry out "man overboard" and create a furor. So, on schedule, Screwy dove over the side of the ship and started

---

* "French out" is midshipman slang for leaving the Naval Academy without authorization.
† Midshipman Hugh Howard "Screwy" Lewis, USN, stood next to last among the 464 graduates in the class of 1934; he retired as a captain in 1962. Midshipman Peyton M. Magruder, USN, left the Naval Academy prior to graduation; he died in 1982.
‡ USS Arkansas (BB-33) was commissioned 17 September 1912. Following modernization in 1925-26 she had a standard displacement of 26,100 tons, was 562 feet long and 106 feet in the beam. Her top speed was 21 knots. She was armed with 12 12-inch guns and 16 5-inch guns. The ship was frequently used for midshipman training cruises in the years between the World Wars.

swimming out, allegedly towards a commercial ship on which he'd met some girls. He was going over there but didn't have the steam to make it.

So, what with everything, the lights went on all over the ship. The movie was over, and after things calmed down, they called a muster. Every midshipman had to get up and be interrogated. Sure enough, nobody knew who had jumped over the side. As far as I know, to this day, he went unpunished. [Laughter]

Q: How would the muster not detect his absence?

Captain Merrill: That's a good question. These were ingenious fellows. I think Screwy got back on board via the boat boom before the muster.

Q: I see.

Captain Merrill: There were ways to defeat the system, and it was a great triumph to get away with a prank like this and increase your reputation. Also, here we are, about 55 years later, as a class talking about this wonderful achievement and laughing about it. Well, that's part of human nature.

Q: Any other of those pranks you recall?

Captain Merrill: Oh, yes, there was the time when Heliodore Aimé Marcoux flung a burning wastebasket out of his room in Bancroft Hall.* Now, his room was right next to mine, and he had a roommate named Red Lennox.† Both of them were just as screwy as you could imagine, but great fellows just the same, and they loved a prank. It was a dark night, and we were all studying in our rooms. All of a sudden, my roommate and I heard a fire engine coming down the street with the sirens going and engine roaring. We looked out

---

* Midshipman Marcoux graduated with the class of 1934.
† Midshipman William R. Lennox, USN, resigned from the Navy on the day of graduation in 1934. He subsequently reached the rank of captain in the Naval Reserve.

the window and saw a fire going on the ground. As it turned out, Heliodore had flung out a wastebasket with some film that was taken during a flight simulating defense against a towed sleeve.

Q: On a gun camera.

Captain Merrill: Yes, a gun camera. So all of this film was given to the midshipmen. Heliodore and Red Lennox put their film in a wastebasket and then concocted this great idea. They put a match to the film and then flung the whole thing out the window. [Laughter]

Then, of course, different people reported the fire, and this great commotion took place. Here, again, I don't think they were pinpointed as the criminals, and I don't know whether a real effort was made. I do know that we got interviewed, as next door neighbors to them, but nobody was about to talk. In the first place, we didn't see what happened. And we didn't have a code of ethics which required us to speculate or report any prank like this. I think that the regimental officer realized that pranks would occur, no matter what. It's indicative, though, of the changing times. Pranks are one thing, but crime is another, and nobody is going to countenance crime at the Naval Academy.

Q: Murder being the most extreme example.

Captain Merrill: Yes.

Q: There's no constructive purpose served by throwing a wastebasket full of burning film out a window. It must have been just to see what they could get away with.

Captain Merrill: Exactly.

Q: What else do you remember about the cruises? Which year would that have been on board the <u>Arkansas</u>?

Captain Merrill: Well, that was our youngster cruise in 1931. I wrote an article for Shipmate on this one.* It covered Sir Hubert Wilkins's aborted attempt to lead a submarine expedition to the North Pole.

Q: I think his submarine was called the Nautilus.

Captain Merrill: Yes, and it broke down in the mid-Atlantic. Two ships, the Arkansas and Wyoming, were sent to rendezvous with it. You probably know the story.

Q: Well, let me hear your version, please.

Captain Merrill: When we got there, we saw this crippled submarine wallowing around in moderate seas. It was evident that you couldn't repair the sub; it had to be towed. Fortunately--for the Arkansas midshipmen at least--the Wyoming was detailed to tow the submarine to Ireland.† We went on and finished our cruise. Thus, for example, we were able to go to Funchal, Madeira, where we had a lot of fun. But Wyoming had to tow this Nautilus to Ireland. So the mids aboard lost a lot of shore leave as a result.

Q: What are your memories of being introduced to shipboard life in the Arkansas?

Captain Merrill: Well, there again, I became guardedly fond of hammocks; my body was young and able to withstand the stresses, and it was comfortable. We had duties there in the engine room, for example, which were unpleasant and hot. Up on deck, it was different. We learned a lot of practical navigation. I'd say the cruise was well worth the Navy's expenditure in money and effort.

---

* Grayson Merrill, "Submarines at the Pole," Shipmate, March 1994, pages 19-20. A copy of the article is included as an appendix at the back of this volume.
† The Wyoming (BB-32) took the disabled Nautilus in tow in mid-June 1931. Sir Hubert Wilkins was a noted British Arctic explorer.

Q: The ship had probably just been converted from coal to oil at that point.

Captain Merrill: That's right.

Q: What do you recall about the messing arrangement? Was that in division messes?

Captain Merrill: Yes. We had mess tables that were put down on the deck under the stowed hammocks. Thus a gun compartment would also serve as a hammock housing area and a mess hall as well. You ate your food wherever you could find a space. The mess attendants would bring up the food and take the used utensils back to the galley.

Q: What do you remember about the gunnery?

Captain Merrill: We actively participated in gunnery. I was a pointer, which was one of the two aiming stations. One guy aimed in elevation and the other in azimuth. They had towed targets, and we shot at them. I don't remember whether we hit any or not; it's still an open question. We had the ship's roll to deal with, requiring a manual skill. If your skill was good, you hit the target, and if it wasn't, you didn't. Just real down-to-earth, fundamental gunnery.

Q: Did you find yourself enjoying shipboard life?

Captain Merrill: Well, no. I knew at the time that I didn't want to spend my life on that ship. I was ready, myself, to accept the idea of being an officer on a ship as a route to promotion and other, more important, duties. But as far as, let's say, an enlisted seaman (which functionally we were) it was a tough life, especially as the months went by, and you were away from your family and all that.

Q: But it gave you an appreciation for their life-style.

Captain Merrill: Exactly.

Q: Any interesting things about the Arkansas's crew that you recall?

Captain Merrill: Not particularly. I didn't have any friendships develop. I admired most of the men that I saw, and I felt that they made their ship a good one.

Q: Well, and it introduced you even more to the hierarchy of the naval setup.

Captain Merrill: Yes. I mean, that's really where the Navy is: on ships in those compartments--eating that food and living that life.

Q: What are your recollections of the liberty ports?

Captain Merrill: When the midshipmen went ashore, their activities depended on their personalities and what they wanted to do. Some of them would go to the museums, some of them would go to the nearest beer joint, and a few of them to houses of ill repute, as the phrase goes. And all those things were available. To me, it was very exciting to be able to go ashore in the Azores, to travel around and see the beauty of the island, and observe how the people lived there.

In my case, going into a casino in Madeira was my first encounter with a roulette system in which "you couldn't lose." In my system you bet either red or black, and if you lost you doubled your bet on the same color. Well, that worked fine for the first day. Then I went back the following day, and the laws of probability caught up with me (in the form of zero or double zero). [Laughter] So I shelled out about $35.00, an awful lot of money in those days. I've been leery of gambling ever since.

Q: That was a good lesson to learn.

Captain Merrill: It was.

Q: Did you get into the Mediterranean at all?

Captain Merrill: Yes, we got as far as Gibraltar. That permitted us to go into an Arab city right across the strait, Tangier, Morocco. That was an eye-opener!

Q: Please tell me about it.

Captain Merrill: You can see it in the movies, and it's pretty realistic. Basically, it's a kind of hubbub of human activity: little shops, people going along on bicycles, beggars wanting your money, and smells. It's something that you want to see once, or at the most, twice, and then you go home.

Q: Much more exotic than Covina.

Captain Merrill: Yes, but I'd go back to Covina any time.

Q: How did you spend the summer of 1932, following your youngster year?

Captain Merrill: Okay, second class summer was spent right here in Annapolis. We were involved with training the plebes quite a bit. It didn't impress me very much, one way or the other. It was something that I had to get through, but I also had two weeks' leave. I drove back to California, and I had some adventures in that respect.

Four midshipman banded together, and we rented a used car. We all lived in southern California. As it turned out, the car was not too dependable. It was an oil eater, for one thing. We had to stock up several gallons of oil that we knew we were going to need. Cars had running boards in those days, including a kind of fence within which you could store baggage. We elected to put the oil on the left-hand running board, and about every 200 miles we'd have to put another quart of oil into the engine.

The second day we got into Kansas, and I was driving at night. I was tired, and my judgment wasn't as good as it should have been. Another car came along with the lights shining up, not down, and I got too close to him. He clipped our running board, and all the oil spread out through our baggage, which was stored aft of it. So I was a very unpopular member of the crew. We got out in the middle of the night and used a flashlight to pick up the clothes that were full of oil and all and threw them into the back. The next day we had to stop and take care of the clothing problem. So we lost a full day doing that. But that was just one incident.

Understandably, the rest of crew said they'd never come back with me. But I had a cousin out in California, so after I had visited my family, his parents decided that driving to Annapolis with me would be very educational for him. In later years he received a better education and became an eminent doctor. At any rate, we drove back, and we had some misadventures, uncomfortable ones, you might say. Fifteen tire punctures later, we arrived in Chicago, and there he gave up.

Q: He had had enough adventure.

Captain Merrill: He had had enough adventure, and he was educated. He said, "You know, you go on ahead and go on back to the Naval Academy, and I'll just get off here in Chicago and take the bus. I've got enough cash from my parents." So we parted company there, and I finally got the rented car back. It was so beat up that, for the next academic year, I kept getting bills from the rental company, which I never paid.

Q: For repairs?

Captain Merrill: For repairs and other scratches and dents that happened.

Q: How long did it take to drive across country in that era?

Captain Merrill: Oh, we figured five days; five days it took, nonstop.

Q: As you made your way across America, what did you observe of the effects of the Depression?

Captain Merrill: Well, to be honest with you, I wasn't as impressed or aware of the Depression as I should have been, simply because I was being paid a living wage--enough to get by. I had saved up enough money to make this trip, and I got back alive, so I didn't really look closely at what I was going through. It was a five-day trip, and I was busy getting the car back and forth from where it should be. But I heard about it as we went along. So I was aware to that degree. I never went hungry, let's say.

Q: Well, you were very fortunate then to be protected against its effects.

Captain Merrill: Yes, in that sense.

Q: Did you get any exposure to naval aviation during your time at the academy?

Captain Merrill: Yes. We had some training planes stationed here. I believe they were seaplanes, and I recall going up for some gunnery practice in them. But that didn't excite me or get me oriented toward aviation. That came later, when I was forced to choose a career after graduation. The ground rules in those days were explicit: "After you graduate, you're going to go out in the surface fleet for two years. Also, you're not going to get married." That was a product of the Depression, and the thought never occurred to us to sue for our civil rights to get married. We just accepted it.

Q: What do you recall about the first-class cruise. What ship was that in?

Captain Merrill: In the summer of 1933 we were new first classmen and stayed at the academy to help train the plebes.

Q: Any specifics on the academics and some of the instructors there?

Captain Merrill: There were some that were challenging. I can remember Walter Diehl, who taught chemistry, and did it very effectively. Then there was "Slipstick Willie," who taught physics with a dramatic flair.* Otherwise, I can't remember any teaching personalities.

Q: And a lot of this was rote learning, just as the prep school had been.

Captain Merrill: Yes, exactly.

Q: Did you have any run-ins with the duty officers in Bancroft?

Captain Merrill: Well, yes, I did. I had one which wasn't a deliberate prank but a stupidity on my part. My graduation weekend, a girlfriend came from California and got here late. There was a dance that was held at the same time as another event, a choral group or something like that. The two of us went to this choral group, which lasted longer than the dance. So I figured that my deadline for getting back into Bancroft Hall was 11:00 o'clock.

When I got back at 11:00, the duty officer greeted me saying, "You're a half hour over the deadline. So go to your room and pack your gear. You're going down to the prison ship." This I did. The Reina Mercedes was the prison ship at that time. What had happened, actually, was that I mistakenly signed up to go to the dance.

I got down to the ship and spent the night there, wondering what the heck was going to happen next, whether I would graduate. I figured they'd let me off since I was graduating two days later. The next day, after breakfast, I looked out between bars on a port and saw a sailboat pass by with a midshipman at the helm and a very attractive girl sitting nearby. As she waved to me, I realized that this was the girl I took to the chorus last

---

* "Slipstick Willie" was the nickname given Professor Earl W. Thomson because of his prowess with a slide rule. He taught at the Naval Academy from 1919 to 1959. For details see Shipmate magazine, published by the Naval Academy Alumni Association, June 1982, page 13.

night. Worse yet, my roommate had been selected to entertain her while I languished in the brig. Well, toward the end of the afternoon, the authorities took pity on me and let me out of the brig. I got back and graduated. [Laughter]

Q: Who was your roommate?

Captain Merrill: Eugene "Pooch" Davis, who's deceased now.[*]

Q: Anything you remember about him as a midshipman?

Captain Merrill: Well, he was a ladies' man, for one thing, unlike me.

Q: It sounds like he was an opportunist also.

Captain Merrill: Exactly. We got along very well, spending four years together as roommates. He went out into the fleet, as I did. But we never saw each other again after that.

Q: Any of your other classmates that you particularly remember as midshipmen?

Captain Merrill: Yes. As my life went on, I became was very friendly with Ernest E. Christensen.[†] His son is now a rear admiral in the Navy.[‡] Anyway, Ernie and I were great friends, and our paths crossed frequently; both of us were involved in guided missile work. Our families were very friendly too. He's deceased now, but his widow, Margie, lives here in Annapolis.[§]

---

[*] Midshipman Eugene W. Davis, USN, who graduated in the class of 1934. He retired as a captain in 1964 and died in 1976.
[†] Midshipman Ernest E. Christensen, USN, graduated in 1934, eventually retired as a rear admiral in 1972.
[‡] Rear Admiral Ernest E. Christensen, Jr., USN, was Commander Training Command, U.S. Atlantic Fleet, at the time of this interview.
[§] Admiral Christensen died 28 March 1988.

Q: The class of 1933 had not all been able to graduate because of the Depression.* Was there a concern that the same thing would happen to your class?

Captain Merrill: Yes there was, in the beginning of 1934, because the impact of FDR and his programs had yet to occur.† That was an election year, '34. What really happened there, I think, is that the whole nation's attitude toward the Depression shifted with FDR. Somehow, he turned the country around, and they said, "Well, that's enough of this Depression. We're going to deal with it instead of moaning about it while downsizing the military and all that sort of thing. We're going to go forward with it."

Then all his programs came into being. Congress asked, "Why did we educate this class of midshipmen if we're going to send half of them home? That makes no sense at all." About halfway through that year, we were all pretty confident that we were going to be commissioned. But in the first half of the year we were fearful that we'd get the same treatment as '33 did.

Q: You said you didn't get involved in sports. I wonder what your memories are of attending sporting events, such as the football games and so forth?

Captain Merrill: Oh, I enjoyed those very much. I got very excited about them, and I thought they were great. That was just youthful exuberance, I suppose. But I think that the impact of sports on midshipmen is good, to get excited about their team and hope the team will win and deal with it if it doesn't. These are good experiences, because that's going to happen in life as they go along.

---

* As an economy measure, in 1933 only the top half of that year's Naval Academy graduating class received Navy and Marine Corps commissions. Some members of the class were subsequently commissioned in 1934 and 1935. Still others joined the reserve and served on active duty in later years. And some were commissioned in other branches of the service.

† FDR--Franklin D. Roosevelt served as President of the United States from 4 March 1933 until his death on 12 April 1945.

Q: And it promotes a bonding among the midshipmen.

Captain Merrill: Exactly. It's beneficial.

Q: And it's especially so since almost all are going into the same business once they graduate.

Captain Merrill: Exactly, the same organization, the same mission and goals. The Naval Academy, in that respect and in many other respects, is unique. Of course, it's not unique to the Army and the Air Force. I would think it would be just awful if those academies were shut down--a great loss to the country.

Q: Well, the fact that you went to a class luncheon 62 years after graduation suggests the bond that was formed.

Captain Merrill: Exactly, I suppose that these things are going on at Harvard and Yale; I don't know. But there's a bond there that's pretty hard to beat.

Q: What do you remember about the marching and drilling as a midshipman?

Captain Merrill: Well, I wouldn't say that they "created a bond." [Laughter] But, there again, it gives you a sense of discipline in a military environment--doing team things, creating a show. A symbolism is involved. You're all in it, the whole regiment is there, you're all in uniform. You've got the flags waving. You're all doing the same thing, and it's a stirring sight. There's something in the human being that responds to a parade. So I think it's good if it's not overdone.

Q: Well, it forces teamwork.

Captain Merrill: Yes.

Q: What do you remember about the graduation of your class?*

Captain Merrill: I don't remember anything about the address. I can't even remember who gave it, because I was busy thinking about what came next. But it was a culmination of events, and, you know, it was a big milestone in our lives. The throwing of the caps and all that is a part of the symbolism. So I marked it just as another event.

Q: Were you eager to get out to that next event and away from the discipline that you'd been involved with?

Captain Merrill: Yes, I was eager for that, because I felt that the four years of dedication and duty were invaluable. But there comes a time, especially in a youngster's life, where he says, "It's time for me to stop going to school for a while and try my wings."

Q: A sense of impatience.

Captain Merrill: Exactly, and I think that's about the right time--when you're 20 years old or so.

Q: How did you get assigned specifically to the West Virginia?†

Captain Merrill: Oh, a detail officer, but I'm sure he did it by the numbers, I don't think there was any particular selection involved.

---

* The graduation was on 31 May 1934. Midshipman Merrill stood number 49 of the 464 graduates in the class.
† USS West Virginia (BB-48) was commissioned 1 December 1923. She had a full-load displacement of 33,590 tons, was 624 feet long and 98 feet in the beam. Her top speed was 21 knots. She was armed with eight 16-inch guns and 12 5-inch broadside guns. She remained in active service until decommissioned on 9 January 1947, following World War II.

Q: But it sounds as if it was not your choice.

Captain Merrill: Oh, definitely not. We just learned somewhere along the line where we were going. We had no voice in our duty assignments in those days.

Q: What are your recollections of reporting to your first ship?

Captain Merrill: Reporting to the West Virginia was just walking up the gangplank, saluting, and saying, "Reporting for duty, sir," or something like that.

Q: Was she at San Pedro at the time?

Captain Merrill: She was in San Pedro, Of course, reporting aboard the first time is something you do with apprehension. You're trained to do it, so you screw up your courage, go up there, and act like you're in complete charge of yourself, which you aren't, of course.

Q: Was the apprehension mainly because it was something different?

Captain Merrill: Yes, probably so. It was completely different for me. I didn't know what kind of assignment I'd get, duty-wise, and I don't think I knew a single soul on the ship. So it's like moving into a new town, I'd say, but different in that you're subject to the discipline of the ship.

Q: What, in fact, were your first assignments when you got on board?

Captain Merrill: I was assigned to engineering. Logically enough, I first spent time learning the physical plant. The chief engineer, Lieutenant Commander Carr, was a very capable officer.[*] I might add that he knew the limitations of his new officers. He had some young

---

[*] Lieutenant Commander T Dewitt Carr, USN.

men who had book learning and knew what a boiler was and how it worked and a turbine and so on. So he put us to work tracing pipelines and, of course, standing watches alongside of somebody who knew what he was doing. We learned the system, but it was rather boring. Also, it was darned uncomfortable; the temperatures ranged between 100 and 125 degrees Fahrenheit. It was something I looked forward to graduating from. [Laughter]

Q: What can you say about the professionalism of the enlisted men in the West Virginia?

Captain Merrill: There were some very professional enlisted men. In those days you'd find enlisted men that had been on a ship in a particular function for 8 to 12 years.

Q: Probably some of the plank owners were still in the crew.*

Captain Merrill: Right, and they were core people, because they knew every nut and bolt in the area in which they worked. They were proud of their jobs. A very essential part of the ship, these old-timers.

Q: One of the skills of a machinist's mate was able to listen to the machinery and tell when there was a problem.

Captain Merrill: Exactly. They proved there's no substitute for experience and hands-on knowledge. That's what these guys had.

Q: Did you become a division officer in time?

Captain Merrill: No, because I was on that ship for only one year, and I spent most of it on extra duties, such as a mess officer for the junior officers' mess. That was unpleasant,

---

* Plank owners is a term that describes the original crew members of a given ship.

because it was nothing but dealing with complaints and the Filipino mess attendants. But, there again, every experience is a lesson.

Q: I interviewed one of your classmates, Admiral Jackson Arnold.* He reported to the Arizona and became the mess treasurer. He said his platform as a candidate was that he would make sure that at least one person was satisfied with every meal, and that was he.

Captain Merrill: [Laughter] Well said.

Q: What were some of the liberty opportunities for junior officers there in Southern California?

Captain Merrill: Well, of course, Southern California, down around the Hollywood, Santa Monica, and San Pedro areas is hard to beat. We enjoyed going ashore. My wife-to-be went to Occidental College, which is just east of Los Angeles. I met her toward the end of the year I was on the West Virginia. My sister, by this time, was also in Occidental College, thanks to the Masons putting her there. My mother was still alive, so I had family life going. I was also entranced by a classmate of my sister.

Q: What was her name?

Captain Merrill: Her name was Mary Elizabeth Wilson at that point, and I managed to change that two years later. Actually, we became reacquainted later in San Diego; she lived in Escondido before going to Occidental.

After one year on West Virginia. I was transferred to the destroyer Brooks in San Diego. I met Mary Elizabeth again at the San Diego World's Fair. She was a customer relations person in a county exhibit of precious stones. She was showing these stones to

---

* Admiral Jackson D. Arnold, USN (Ret.). This interview was used in the book Battleship Arizona (Annapolis: Naval Institute Press, 1991).

people, and I pretended to be very interested and asked her about this and that. She didn't recognize me at first, probably because I was in uniform.

Finally I screwed up my courage and asked her what she was doing after she left the job. She said, well, she had an engagement, but it depended. The engagement would be over in about an hour or so, and if I could meet with her after that she could deal with this other engagement. So I waited, met her, and things went on from there.

Q: Well, naval officers had a fair degree of social status at the time.

Captain Merrill: Yes, they did. It didn't take me long to tell her where we met before and who I was.

Q: And somebody with a steady job would be appealing as well.

Captain Merrill: That's right.

Q: Do you remember the skipper from the West Virginia, Captain Stark?[*]

Captain Merrill: Yes. I do remember him. Of course, later on, he became a famous admiral, and he was a most able person.[†] However, he was at the top of the ship's social structure and the top of the military structure as well. Although I saw him in passing, so to speak, I never had very much conversation with him. We had, I suppose, 1,000 people on the ship, and he had to deal with all of them.

Q: Did you make the obligatory call on the skipper?

---

[*] Captain Harold R. Stark, USN, commanded the USS West Virginia (BB-48) from 14 December 1933 to 17 October 1934.
[†] As a four-star admiral, Stark was Chief of Naval Operations, 1939-42.

Captain Merrill: I think we did, as a group, but he had an executive officer who was more domineering and more a focus of the social activities of the ship.

Q: Commander Shafroth?

Captain Merrill: That's right, Jack Shafroth had an eligible daughter.[*] He was a giant of a man, both literally and professionally.

Q: Probably 300 pounds.

Captain Merrill: Yes, fortunately his daughter didn't come up to that weight, but she was a big-hearted and able-bodied woman, I'll tell you. I got acquainted with her, and we attended several affairs together. We didn't have any emotional attachment at all, of course.

One of the things that happened to me on the <u>West Virginia</u> was getting appendicitis. My dad died of that, so I was a little concerned, and this hit me during the night. I stumbled my way up to sick bay, which was in the forward part of the ship, and a corpsman laid me out on a bunk. In the morning, when the doctors arrived, they quickly diagnosed my problem as appendicitis. So off I went to the hospital in Bremerton. Jack Shafroth's daughter came up and visited with me, comforted me after the operation.

Q: Had the appendix ruptured?

Captain Merrill: No, it was a timely and successful operation. My father died of a ruptured appendix when I was four. He was on a trip and got as far as Bakersfield. The doctor there was incompetent, they told me, and he died, so I was concerned about it,

Q: Understandably.

Captain Merrill: Anyway, that worked out fine.

---

[*] Commander John F. Shafroth, Jr., USN.

Q: Did you have a flag embarked on the ship when you were on board?

Captain Merrill: I don't think we did,

Q: Any memories from the overhaul in Bremerton?*

Captain Merrill: One of the things I can remember is standing a miserable watch on deck in the pelting rain and sleet that's famous for Bremerton in the winter. Otherwise, we went in, had our stuff fixed, and went back out again. How did you happen to know about that?

Q: Well, it must have a yard period, if you were in Bremerton. I can't think of another reason to go there.

Captain Merrill: Okay, you got me. [Laughter]

Q: I stood officer-of-the-deck watches in Bremerton in 1969 on board the New Jersey, and I remember that steady rain. It would puddle in the canvas we had over the quarterdeck. So periodically I'd take the OOD's long glass and push up on the canvas and coax the water overboard.†

Captain Merrill: That's typical.

Q: What do you remember about the ship's operating pattern?

Captain Merrill: I remember gunnery practices, in particular. Again, the gunnery was pretty elemental. They'd get out there with a towed raft and fire 16-inch shells at it. It's pretty impressive stuff. I look at it now, in retrospect, that we were too satisfied with those guns. We thought, well, if World War II comes along--and there was talk of that at the time--that

---

* Puget Sound Navy Yard, Bremerton, Washington.
† OOD--officer of the deck.

everything was in pretty good shape. As far as the main battery was concerned they were, but on the West Virginia they were thinking of the World War I battles, where you had a line of battleships here and another line there. Of course, destroyers would break through the smoke screen for a torpedo attack, but the 5-inch guns would take care of that. That's the way they were thinking from a gunnery point of view.

Few battlewagon officers were thinking about an airplane dive-bombing on their ship, and that's where their weakness lay until Pearl Harbor.

Q: Were there antiaircraft practices?

Captain Merrill: There were, but they'd tow a sleeve by and the machine gunners would shoot at the sleeve. If they hit it four or five times, "Well done."

They used to have competitions in the battleships. That's how they ranked the ships; the whole effort was to win the competition and fly the "meat ball."[*] So the whole effort, in the case of gunnery, was to get a higher score than the other battleships. Nobody was asking how good these guns would be in a real war. In retrospect, somebody should have been thinking about it, but they didn't. Realistic targets were lacking.

Q: That situation that you described is a definition for complacency, it sounds like.

Captain Merrill: Exactly. Later on there were things that happened with target drones that dramatized this deficiency.

Q: Did you have inklings, say, in the mid-'30s, that Japan would be a future opponent?

Captain Merrill: Yes, I think so. In fact, if you wanted to define it, if we had anything like a cold war at that time, it was with Japan. They had the other Navy; the Germans didn't.

---

[*] The "meat ball" was the nickname for the battle efficiency pennant awarded to the ship that stood best in annual competition.

They had it, and they were an Axis power, so where else would war come from? Yes, it seemed clear to me, at that point, that Japan was our probable enemy.

Q: Did you get time on the bridge in the West Virginia?

Captain Merrill: Yes, some, not as much as I'd like. I was only there one year, and I was in the engineering department almost all of that year. But once in a while I was up on the bridge.

Q: What are your recollections of the station keeping and turning in the exact spot the ship ahead turned?

Captain Merrill: Well, there was great emphasis on it. Again, the focus was to win the competition, to look best, for example, to turn in the same spot or keep the right distance between you and the ship ahead. When I went into destroyers in the next year, I had an experience with this; it's a sea story. If you want me to tell it, I will.

Q: Oh, please do.

Captain Merrill: Okay. I went first in one destroyer, the Brooks and later the Dorsey. The Brooks was in a war game.* There were two lines of battleships, and the "enemy destroyers" laid a smoke screen to protect their battle line from a torpedo attack. Our job was to penetrate the screen in column, upon emerging turn and launch torpedoes, then continue turning and retire back through the screen. Brooks was number four in the column.

---

* USS Brooks (DD-232), a Clemson-class destroyer, was commissioned 18 June 1920. Standard displacement was 1,215 tons, length 314 feet, and beam of 32 feet. Top speed was 35 knots. She was armed with four 5-inch guns, one 3-inch gun, and 12 21-inch torpedo tubes.

I was the OOD with the skipper standing "on alert" in the bridge wing.* The first three ships disappeared into the screen and did their thing. Then we penetrated and emerged, only to see the division leader charging directly at us at some 22 knots. Obviously, he had turned more than 180 degrees, but there was no time to argue. I called out "right full rudder" and "all engines full astern." The skipper saw a different solution and yelled "left full rudder." He did not formally relieve me as OOD; there was no time for that since we shortly went roaring by each other at a separation of some 20 yards!

After we had safely avoided the other two ships, the skipper turned to the ever-present mess attendant and said, "Joe, go below and get me a cup of the blackest damned coffee you can find." I hate to put it this way, but there were a lot of soiled britches on the bridge and in the engine room that day!

Q: I understand your meaning.

Captain Merrill: So, that's the kind of thing that went on in those days. I'm not detracting from that, but I am wandering away from the prewar mind-set that we were previously talking about.

Q: Well, there was intense competition in the engineering plants as well.

Captain Merrill: Exactly, yeah. So I don't know, maybe the idea was that there should be more simulations of situations like this collision, but it's best to do those on simulators, I guess.

Q: Well, I've gotten the impression that sometimes these competitions were almost ends in themselves.

Captain Merrill: Yes, they were.

---

* The commanding officer of the Brooks was then Lieutenant Commander Charles F. Fielding, USN.

Q: You talked about the junior officer mess. I've heard of some ships in which that was essentially a fraternity house atmosphere. Was it like that in the West Virginia?

Captain Merrill: Yes, I would say so. There were young guys in there, and there was a little horseplay that went on, but less so than midshipmen. Midshipmen are just youngsters, but in the junior officers' mess, for example, you'd find probably half of them were married. They had families, and that changes your attitude toward horsing around.

Q: But still not as much decorum as in the wardroom.

Captain Merrill: Oh, no, nowhere near that. We were glad to be by ourselves.

Q: Did you get any liberty in any of the other ports on the West Coast?

Captain Merrill: Well, not in West Virginia. But when I was in destroyers, we went into San Diego. Liberty in San Diego was quite like it was up in the Los Angeles area, except maybe better because Los Angeles was beginning to get sprawled. San Diego did not start that until later.

Q: Well, it was very compact with Broadway coming up right from the fleet landing.

Captain Merrill: Right. It was a small town.

Q: Any other recollections from the West Virginia to put on the record?

Captain Merrill: Well, I reckoned it as one of the best battleships in the division. Again, maybe my judgment was affected by this "measured" competition. But it was a well-run ship. Captain Stark and Jack Shafroth were good leaders. There were good people on the ship, both enlisted and officers. I liked that ship.

Q: Well, she was then the newest battleship, and I think a plum assignment for officers.

Captain Merrill: Yes.

Q: What do you remember about the spit-and-polish atmosphere?

Captain Merrill: I don't feel that it was overdone. The implication of those words is that there's too much of it. But I don't think the West Virginia had too much. It was a clean ship. It was well painted and kept up, but, more importantly, there were very few breakdowns in the machinery that I can remember. Of course, it was new.

Q: Any recollections of the aircraft that the ship operated?

Captain Merrill: Yes, I can remember them being catapulted off the after gun turret. The name of one of the pilots was Horney.* He was something of a typical stereotype aviator in that he liked to show off now and then. He loved to land in heavy seas, kissing the crest of each wave as it went underneath until he could finally land on the down slope of an easy one. I can remember the others too; they did a good job. All they did, of course, was go up and spot gunfire or go out on a scouting mission. They did it and did it well.

Q: Was there any appeal from those planes to you going into aviation?

Captain Merrill: Probably, there was a glamour to aviation in those days. That was the coming thing in the Navy, and everybody sensed it. Of course, of the carriers that we had, only the Saratoga was operating there, at that time. We saw very little of the Lexington, the other operational carrier. The old Langley was a training ship. So aviation hadn't gotten very far. But there was a conviction in the minds of young, ambitious officers that if they could be aviators, they wanted to do it.

---

* Lieutenant (junior grade) Harry R. Horney, USN.

Q: Did you go up for rides in the back seat at all?

Captain Merrill: Not on the West Virginia. I would have enjoyed it. I had a unique experience while in San Diego visiting my girlfriend. A classmate, who was stationed on the submarine Bonita, contacted me. He said, "Why don't you come on out and enjoy an experience on a submerged submarine?"

So I said, "Sure, let's go." I went out on this exercise where we dived and stayed under for about an hour. The ship began to get hot and stinky. I decided, "Well, this is it. I'm going to be an aviator," and I did. It was pretty awful down there. Of course, I realize that nowadays it's a different ball game in submarines.

Q: Far, far different.

Captain Merrill: Yes. But that's the kind of decision-making that happens with a young person.

Q: Captain, we've talked briefly on your life in the destroyers. Could you go into some more detail on the Brooks, please.

Captain Merrill: The Brooks was commanded by a mustang lieutenant commander.* Like most mustangs, he was a most able person, lots of experience, common sense, and devoted to his job. And I learned a great deal from him. Amongst other things, the father of my upcoming wife came out, unbeknownst to me, to the ship and interviewed him to make sure that I was a suitable husband for his daughter.

Q: [Laughter] Did the captain give you a good recommendation?

---

* "Mustang" is Navy slang for a former enlisted man who has risen through the ranks to become an officer. Such was the case for Lieutenant Commander Fielding.

Captain Merrill: As it turned out. Of course, all this was unbeknownst to me, but I got a lesson from it. If I had been the father of a girl, which I never became, this is what I'd do. Apparently I passed the test. I was great friends with the skipper and learned a lot from him.

Q: Such as?

Captain Merrill: Well, mostly about watch standing on a destroyer, which is a different ball game than a battleship. Things happen fast up there, often times at 20 to 25 knots. The agility of the destroyer and its mission require a "seaman's eye" to stay out of trouble. You don't have bearings coming in all the time. You have to react to the situation as it develops. You don't have radar. You just have what you see and what experience tells you might come up all of a sudden, especially out of smoke, fog or darkness.

Q: Well, you have to be able to anticipate, too, at that kind of speed.

Captain Merrill: Exactly. So that's the kind of thing that I learned there.

After I had been on board for a while, the Brooks was scheduled to transfer to the Atlantic. I didn't want to go then, so I exchanged positions with another ensign. I wound up on the destroyer Dorsey, which was going to stay in the Pacific.* I was waiting out my girlfriend's graduation and the two years' restriction to get married.

Moving on to Dorsey, I'd like to tell about a memorable cruise during a war game going down the Pacific Coast of Mexico, where there are a lot of sea turtles. As a destroyer, we made a simulated attack and were wiped out (constructively). We were told to keep clear of the fleet and let them get on with the war game. Well, our skipper decided to capture a sea turtle and disguise the operation as a man-overboard drill. The crew found a net big enough to handle one of these sea turtles. Then we went searching for a shipmate

---

* USS Dorsey (DD-117), a Rathburne-class destroyer, was commissioned 16 September 1918. Displacement was 1,090 tons, length 314 feet, beam of 32 feet, and draft of 9 feet. Top speed was 35 knots. She was armed with four 4-inch guns, two 3-inch guns, and 12 21-inch torpedo tubes.

overboard. On sighting a turtle we called off the search, hove to, and lowered a boat. Off went the crew and came back with a handsome sea turtle. After admiring the turtle and wishing him Godspeed in the next world, he was slaughtered, and we ate him. [Laughter]

Q: I've never had turtle. What does it taste like?

Captain Merrill: Oh, it's great. It's white meat, this one, anyway, and it was delicious. It was like a big turkey, you might say, just as good too.

Q: Well, that kind of skipper, who's got an element of fun and playfulness about him, is great to serve with.[*]

Captain Merrill: Exactly. He relieves the tension, you know, and builds spirit in the ship, We were lucky.

Q: Well, and inevitably you're going to have more togetherness in a crew in a ship that is small compared with, say, the West Virginia.

Captain Merrill: Exactly,

Q: What do you remember about living conditions on board a four-piper?

Captain Merrill: Whew! Well, one glaring memory I have was at the end of this war game, we put in at a port on the Pacific side of the Panama Canal. My "cabin," if you want to call it that, was extremely small. The bunk was something like 12 inches under some steam pipes that went up to the anchor windlass, and it was hot. I will never forget trying to go to sleep up there. There was some air pumped up there, but it was still pretty miserable.

---

[*] Lieutenant Commander Benton W. Decker, USN, was then the commanding officer of the Dorsey.

Q: So you had primarily steam-operated machinery rather than electrical?

Captain Merrill: Yes, in this particular case,

Q: Any other ship-handling experiences from that ship?

Captain Merrill: No, not that I can come up with. I will say that the war games were a continuous way of life out there. You'd have a couple of them each year, and they involved a cruise, as well as the war games.

Q: Well, and sometimes those were an avenue for experimentation and doctrinal things.

Captain Merrill: Yes, although I think most of us junior officers were not conscious of that. The planners would plan out the battle and different exercises, as you say, to get more tactical experience and knowledge and learn from doing. We were pretty busy with the doing.

Q: Well, for example, though, the lesson was learned that there was a deficiency in antiaircraft gunnery.

Captain Merrill: Yes, but the lesson came with the advent of radio-controlled target drones, not with war games per se.

Q: You described the sense of apprehension you had in going to the West Virginia. Had you, by this time, gotten much more confident?

Captain Merrill: Somewhat, yes. I think that self-confidence grows in you with age and experience. When you're a kid, you're brand new to situations. The only way you can get self-confidence is to face situations, deal with them, and come out feeling that you did a pretty fair job. That's the progress of self-confidence.

Q: Did you get experience taking the ship in and out of port?

Captain Merrill: Especially on the Dorsey, yes. The skipper was very good at letting his officers of the deck at least think they were in charge of the ship. He would be nearby, and he'd leap into a situation where he felt there was danger. But he did permit us to do ship handling coming into port--dealing with other ships passing by. I think he let me make dock landings a couple of times, when there wasn't too much wind blowing and current flowing.

Q: Well, it's useful to let a junior officer make his mistakes so he can learn from them.

Captain Merrill: Right, as long you don't tear up the pier in the process.

Q: Any recollections of gunnery from the destroyers?

Captain Merrill: Well, not any more than what I've said. The guns were World War I vintage. They did what they could do, but, of course, things had changed. Everything on the old four-pipers was okay for World War I, but the ships were overage as far as what was coming up, no question about it. I guess somebody realized that when they did this 50-ship deal for Great Britain.[*] That was good for Britain and for us, too, because it created a ship deficit that the bean counters could use to ask for more money. But they were old ships, and you saw that. There was corrosion. We had leakage in the shaft alleys to deal with. Sometimes a big rust spot would fail, and then you had a water-handling problem. I was glad to see the Navy get new destroyers as time went on.

---

[*] In September 1940 President Franklin D. Roosevelt concluded a deal with Prime Minister Winston Churchill of Great Britain whereby the United States transferred 50 destroyers to the Royal Navy for use against German submarines. In return the United States received 99-year leases to British bases in the West Indies, Bermuda, and Newfoundland.

Grayson Merrill #1 - 45

Q: Well, actually, they started coming out about that time, the so-called gold-platers.*

Captain Merrill: That's right, they did. There may have been one or two new destroyers in the fleet at that point, but most of them were the old four-pipers.

Q: Did you have problems with the reliability of the machinery?

Captain Merrill: Yes, mostly due to old age, corrosion, and things like that.

Q: On the other hand, the fixes were probably simpler. You could make a part in a machine shop, as opposed to needing electronic widgets.

Captain Merrill: That's right. You'd go into a shipyard, and they'd just weld in a new section of hull or whatever they had to do. It was simple, like a Model-T Ford, you might say.

Q: Did you get out to Hawaii in those years?

Captain Merrill: Let's see. During the two years we're talking about, I didn't get out that far. We worked out of the West Coast ports during those two years,

Q: What specific jobs did you have in the destroyers?

Captain Merrill: Well, of course, we had multiple jobs. I was the communications officer and probably the mess treasurer. I can't remember beyond that--probably one more assignment.

Q: And my guess is that the communications were relatively sparse in that era.

---

* The first of the "gold-platers," the modern destroyers designed in the 1930s, was the USS Farragut (DD-348), commissioned 18 June 1934.

Captain Merrill: They were. Radio was handicapped by its vacuum tubes--low reliability, and no high-frequency stuff there. All Morse code, of course.

Q: Well, the encryption and decryption were pretty laborious in that era, weren't they?

Captain Merrill: Oh, they were. You just had a code book to that you worked with. It was very elemental.

Q: Well, and then a higher proportion of communications then were done visually, as opposed to radio.

Captain Merrill: That's true.

Q: Tactical signals.

Captain Merrill: We had blinker signals, we had flag signals, and all tactics depended on these. They did all right as long as the ships were in sight of each other. But where they lacked communication was in the long-distance category. My memory is that they did not have ship-to-ship voice radio. I'm not sure of that, but I think that's true.

Q: How did you juggle your shipboard duties with the budding romance during that period?

Captain Merrill: Well, the division of effort there was pretty clear. When you were on the ship at sea, romance went out the window. When you were in port, you had a certain amount of time for liberty, and you used it to best advantage.

Of course, my girlfriend was up in Occidental College. I can remember one time going up there. Now, my sister was a sorority mate of hers, and that's how I originally got acquainted with her. Our next meeting was this gem thing in San Diego. Thereafter my sister promoted the romance pretty well for me. So my wife-to-be was in the same sorority building. I remember going up to visit her, and I thought I'd pull a prank. The whole sorority knew that I was coming up and that I was this hotshot ensign from a destroyer courting her.

As I drove up in front of the sorority, I could see the window shades were open and people looking out. So I got out of my car and deliberately limped up to the front door so that I looked like a cripple. [Laughter] She came to the door and snatched me inside. That was the whole prank, but it was all that was needed to start a rumor that their sorority sister was going to marry this cripple from the Navy. Fortunately, she had a sense of humor, and the truth came out at the dance that night.

Q: What sorts of things would you do on dates, for example?

Captain Merrill: What did we do? Generally speaking, we would make a big thing of going to a musical. I can remember going to Grauman's Chinese Theater, a Beverly Hills mecca, even then. It featured musical comedies as well as first-run movies.

Q: Sort of the old vaudeville era.

Captain Merrill: Yes, it was that type of thing. I particularly remember "The Desert Song." You probably never heard of "The Desert Song."

Q: I've heard of it, but that's about as far as it goes.

Captain Merrill: It was built around melodic, romantic music sung by truly pitched voices with much expression. The cast had its good guys, bad guys but no psychos. That was a typical date for me.

Of course, you'd always try to drive up in the mountains above the city after the show. The terms of engagement were well known and abided by. Girls were presumed to be "young ladies" unless they chose not to be. You might even get to necking, but that's as far as it went.

Q: Were these destroyers based in San Diego?

Captain Merrill: Yes, both of them were.

Q: And they didn't have the super highways then, so it was probably a longer drive then than now.

Captain Merrill: Oh, it was. I guess it would take three or four hours. If you averaged 45 miles an hour, you were doing just fine. There was one hazard on the way up called Torrey Pines. It was a steep, winding road. If your car could make it up and over that, you were in.

Q: When did you then get married?

Captain Merrill: We got married in June of '36, two years almost to the day after I graduated, and some of her sorority sisters were there.

Q: Where were you married?

Captain Merrill: At my sister-in-law's home, which, at that time, was in Eagle Rock. It was a home wedding with all the trimmings. I had four friends, ensigns, complete with swords, white gloves, etc. After the wedding we set off in a used car and started back to flight training at Pensacola, Florida. By prearrangement we honeymooned the first night at the Del Mar Hotel just north of San Diego. The next day we started east through Arizona, New Mexico, etc. Shall I move along chronologically?

Q: Yes, please.

Captain Merrill: From both a family and career point of view, getting married and setting off in the heat of a southwest summer toward Pensacola was a milestone for both of us. Ahead was our first house, new friends, flight training and adjusting to life as a married couple--a frightening assignment in retrospect.

After we arrived in Pensacola, we began to sense that we were in sympathetic company. Perhaps 60 of my classmates trickled in, most of them with new wives facing the same problems that we did. Friendships were swiftly formed, some transposing to fellow renters of duplexes and condominiums. This created a wonderful social environment, because we were all in the same boat. There weren't any kids yet, and we had to go out and find rentals. The Merrills teamed up with the Stones in a duplex bordering a nearby bayou. Our friendship with the Stones lasted for many years. He's still alive and retired from the Navy.* Today he's a well-known portrait artist up in Pennsylvania.

Q: Did you encounter any resistance when you applied for flight training?

Captain Merrill: Not resistance exactly, but discouraging advice that I was probably going to have a short life, and also that the way to promotion in the Navy was via surface ships. This came from the old-timers that I've described before. I didn't pay very much attention to it. But that's the only adverse reaction that I can think of to my decision to go into aviation.

Q: What were the factors that brought about your decision?

Captain Merrill: Well, my first diving experience in a submarine narrowed the options. But subsequently I began to see these airplanes flying their missions, especially there in San Diego where they were practicing dive bombing. The first F4B fighters were coming in at that point, and they made an awesome racket when they dove down. But, more

---

* Ensign Lester J. Stone, USN, was a Naval Academy classmate of Merrill. Stone eventually retired as a captain in 1964.

importantly, I could see that these guys were hitting small targets with their inert bombs. It was quite evident to me that large ships were headed for trouble, that aviation was a potent thing in the Navy. There were a lot of things that aviation didn't have, at that point, but they would get someday. I wasn't thinking guided missiles at that time, but I felt that aviation was at the forefront of technology, and that's the way I wanted to go.

Q: Was a sense of adventure any part of your motivation?

Captain Merrill: Of course. All of the live wires in my class, as I viewed them, were either in or going towards aviation or wished they had. There was a general consensus that that was a great career. There was also a realization that your chances of surviving had to be factored in. You couldn't get life insurance, for example, at that particular point. So the Navy paid a bonus "flight pay" of 50% base pay.

Q: That's interesting.

Captain Merrill: Later, life insurance became available through Navy Mutual Aid.

Q: Well, evidently you were able to put that concern aside.

Captain Merrill: Yes, When you are young especially, you push aside the things that might happen. You're more concerned with the things that you think will happen. I don't know how to express it.

Q: Well, it's sort of sense of fatalism that if it's going to happen, it will, but in the meantime, you're going to do it.

Captain Merrill: Right. Have a short and merry life, trade that for a dull, long life.

Q: On the other hand, you've have the benefit of both, an interesting long life.

Captain Merrill: I've been very, very lucky. I've had some hairy experiences, but we'll get into that later.

Q: Please tell me about your initial experiences in flight training.

Captain Merrill: Okay. I was pretty successful in my instruction. Progress was measured by "check flights;" if you got a "down," that was trouble. You had to redo the maneuvers that were ordered and prove that you could do them. I had only one down and that was awarded by Ensign Gage, a very tough instructor who turned me down during a cut-throttle check.[*] I was cruising along at about 2,000 feet where my job was to be ready for a simulated engine failure. I periodically looked around to see where I could land the airplane safely or at least survive.

When the instructor cut the throttle, I had already picked out a grassy strip, a kind of avenue between some trees that was maybe 100 feet wide, say, three or four times the wingspan of the airplane. I figured, "I can glide down there and land on that strip." Well, he didn't think that was the best thing to do, but he let me go ahead and try it. So I glided down and started to land. Some dead tree limbs came into view on the grass ahead. Unless Gage opened the throttle, we would wipe out the landing gear, if not worse. With seconds to go, he pushed the throttle forward and away we went.

My extra-sensory system told me he did not like my performance, and he confirmed this by the classical thumbs-down signal he gave me on the return to base. In retrospect, I think the instructors believed every student needed at least one down check to avoid overconfidence. Anyhow, I repeated the check a week later with another instructor and regained my self-esteem.

Q: What aircraft were you flying?

---

[*] Ensign Kenneth L. Gage, USNR.

Captain Merrill: It was an NT, a bi-wing rotary engine, two-seater built by the Naval Aircraft Factory.

Q: Did you find yourself enjoying the exhilaration of flying?

Captain Merrill: Oh, yes. You know, just to be up there, to be solely in charge of the plane. During my first solo flight, I was the king of the world.

Q: How long did that flight last?

Captain Merrill: Oh, about 30 minutes. It came after some ten hours of dual flight in Squadron One NK seaplanes. After giving a thumbs-up sign, the instructor got out and said, "Okay, you get in, you're solo."

Q: How soon in the training sequence did that appear?

Captain Merrill: After about ten hours of flight, From then on, you didn't concern yourself with solo. You did two-seater instructions, including acrobatics and gunnery and everything else with an instructor in the back. He flew in the back seat as both an instructor and a safety factor. At some point along the way, of course, you got into seaplanes and single-seat fighters. Solo flight was no longer a novelty.

Q: And you probably got introduced to the different types of planes also.

Captain Merrill: Yes. We flew fighters, torpedo bombers, and seaplanes--all the basic types. As a matter of fact, I flew in a TG torpedo bomber there. Later I went to the Saratoga, and flew the same darned airplane off the carrier's deck.

Q: Was there a ground school component to this training also?

Captain Merrill: Yes, there was, we trained in communications, learning Morse code. We also had instructions to familiarize us with the engines and landing gear and the carrier gear that we were going to see, like catapults, retrieving equipment, and so forth. We got a familiarization program. It was a good one too.

Q: Were you warned against the flat-hatting and showing off and so forth?

Captain Merrill: Yes. Despite warnings, the Navy had a certain amount of that, because venturesome people would go ahead and do it anyway. But I didn't do much of it. By that time I was married and had a certain amount of self-control; I was a little older too.

Q: And I've heard that having a wife at home can be an inhibiting factor for aviators.

Captain Merrill: Yes. If my wife heard that I had been flat-hatting around, it wouldn't have advanced our marriage one bit.

Q: [Laughter] How long did it take, in this process, to get your wings?

Captain Merrill: Just over one year. I think it was in August 1937. We reported in June of the previous year.

Q: Another thing that usually cropped up at the three-year mark was studying for promotion exams. Do you recall those?

Captain Merrill: Yes, I do recall them. I had to take those exams, and I lost a few numbers in the process. I wasn't in flight training. I think I was aboard ship, at that point.

Q: I see.

Captain Merrill: Again, it was the same old stuff. We were tested in Navy Regs, ship handling, navigation, etc. And although I had actually been doing these things, I didn't have enough time really to study the books. Because of this, I dropped a few numbers. But it didn't matter in the end.

Q: A few numbers in your class standing?

Captain Merrill: Yes, they rearranged the class standings as a result of those tests.

Q: Well, you talked about graduation from the Naval Academy as a milestone. Certainly getting your wings would be another.

Captain Merrill: Yes, definitely.

Q: Where to from there? Was that then to the Saratoga squadron?

Captain Merrill: Yes. Then I went to the Saratoga. I was in VT-3.[*] My skipper's name was Lieutenant Commander Marion E. Crist, USN. I started off in TG-1 torpedo bombers.[†] The TG-1 was like a big box kite: bi-wing, with one big rotary engine. Three seats in line held a gunner/bombardier, the pilot, and the rear gunner/communicator. The latter had a certain amount of radio equipment--Morse code, naturally--but no voice. A lot of things were lacking that would have been nice to have. But, for its time, it was a good aircraft. I don't recall any mishaps we had or heard of. We were scheduled to get new

---

[*] VT-3--Torpedo Squadron Three.
[†] TG was the designation for a biplane torpedo bomber built by the Great Lakes Aircraft Corporation. Great Lakes had taken over the Glenn L. Martin company's Cleveland plant, so the Martin T4M was redesignated TG. The TG-2 model had a wing span of 53 feet, length of 35 feet, gross eight of 9,236 pounds, and top speed of 127 miles per hour. It was armed with a .30-caliber machine gun in the rear cockpit.

TBDs from Douglas, and it was only a few months after that when they arrived.* Of course, we were all excited.

Q: That was one of the first monoplanes in the fleet.

Captain Merrill: Exactly, and we were conscious of that.

Q: How would you compare the handling characteristics of the two?

Captain Merrill: By automobile analogy, the TG-1 was a light school bus, while the TBD was a sports car. The TG would respond to every gust of wind and would fly along in a jerky fashion. The TBD just flew steadily through the gusts; somehow, it was more stable. It was easy to handle too. However, it had folding wings to save deck space. These were extended and mechanically locked by the pilot before takeoff. Several pilots failed to lock them and crashed. My friend Lester Stone was the only one who survived.

Q: Well, your sports car analogy suggests it had more power too.

Captain Merrill: It did, definitely. It had more speed, but characteristically we'd fly a mission at about 140 knots. For that time we thought that was great stuff, but the fighters were doing far better. The F4Bs were clearly faster. I had a couple of experiences with TBDs that were on the hairy side.

The TBD received its fuel through a capped fitting on the top of each wing. Unbeknownst to me, the Saratoga sailor who fueled up the airplane failed to put the cap back on the port fitting. I was assigned a scouting mission, was catapulted off, and

---

* The TBD Devastator, built by the Douglas Aircraft Company, was a monoplane torpedo bomber. The TBD-1 model had a wing span of 50 feet, length of 35 feet, gross eight of 10,194 pounds, and top speed of 206 miles per hour. It was armed with two .30-caliber machine guns. The first TBD-1 reached squadron VT-3 on 5 October 1937, and the following year was introduced to VT-2, VT-5, and VT-6.

everything seemed fine. On the way back I happened to look out and saw a gaping hole in the top of the wing where the cap should have been.

By this time, the TBDs had voice radio. Worried about a possible fire upon landing, I reported the situation to the ship. They decided that I was to fly until I was darn near out of gas. [Laughter] So while all the other aircraft landed on the ship, I kept circling and circling. I had a gauge to go by, and I'd report periodically how much I had left. When reporting one eighth of a tank, it was with undisguised tension in my voice. Finally they said, "Okay, bring it in." Then in I came, making a normal arrested landing. The trouble was that all the gas remaining sloshed forward and created an inflammable fountain.

Q: Like a geyser.

Captain Merrill: Yes, so after I landed, here's the engine idling hot exhaust gasses back onto a mass of gasoline mixed with air. The result was a huge ball of fire that flared up. It was somewhat disturbing, but the odd thing was it didn't burn anything. With 20 knots of wind over the deck, it was just one big flash which dissipated just astern. Later I had a chat with the captain; both of us were admittedly unnerved by the incident.

Q: Well, that's kind of spectacular.

Captain Merrill: It was spectacular, all right.

Q: We haven't mentioned your getting into the process of learning to land on a carrier deck. How did that come about?

Captain Merrill: The fundamentals of training for carrier landings were taught using an airstrip simulating a carrier deck. It was located at Otay Mesa, just south of San Diego. I trained there with the TG-1 and later graduated to landing on the Saratoga.

At Otay Mesa you learned to make accurate spot landings by obeying signals from a landing signals officer. You made them with your landing gear down, of course, and each landing would be "touch and go"--not arrested as aboard ship. After several days of such simulation, most pilots were deemed ready to try it at sea.

Q: Do you remember a sense of apprehension before your first one?

Captain Merrill: Of course. Your first carrier landing involves getting over some psychological hurdles. Most of us had seen movies of aborted crash landings, and they are not reassuring. But carrier pilots have to summon up the required degree of fatalism and self confidence that the profession demands. As FDR put it, "We have nothing to fear but fear itself." That process is what I went through, and it worked perfectly well. I never made any landings with severe damage. Some were better than others, but at least I always caught the wire.

Q: And your training kicks in.

Captain Merrill: Yes, your training kicks in and takes all your attention. But there are those in naval aviation that can't get rid of the apprehension. I knew two or three guys who turned in their suits voluntarily for that very reason.

Q: Was the Saratoga the first ship you made a landing on?

Captain Merrill: Yes, I was on there for approximately a year. In the meantime, I had put in for postgraduate training, shortly after I joined TorpRon 3. Here again, I was advised not to do it because "You're going to become a numbers cruncher or technology specialist," etc. What I requested was aeronautical engineering, because that was the dominant technology at that point. Another option was electrical engineering (electronics was just a sub-category then), and I put that down as my second choice. I was very disappointed when I received the news that I was not selected for aeronautical engineering. As it turned out, getting my second choice was the best thing that ever happened to me professionally.

Q: Well, before we get to that, maybe you could tell me a little more about the squadron life. What do you remember about the tactics for making an approach to drop a torpedo?

Captain Merrill: We trained in that, of course, sometimes in formation and sometimes in solo. There really wasn't anything mysterious about it, because all you do is fly just above the water, arm the torpedo, and then drop it at the release point. As I remember it, we had a plotter we called an "is-was" that the second-seat guy used to work out the lead angle and release point. Obviously, you're shooting at a moving ship, and you've got to lead it. Knowing the torpedo's speed and estimating the ship's course and speed, the "is-was" gave you desired lead angles as you approached. Choosing the drop point depended on the torpedo's range, enemy countermeasures, and patience.

Rarely would you have a ship target and set the torpedo to go under it. That was too hairy, because sometimes the torpedo insisted on being too close to the surface. Usually we trained against boats or towed targets.

Q: Did you drop exercise torpedoes?

Captain Merrill: Oh, yes. They were expensive to prepare, retrieve, and restore to ready status. I probably didn't drop more that four to six such exercise torpedoes in the year I was there.

Later, in the Battle of Midway, my squadron was totally shot down by enemy fighters before they could launch torpedoes.[*] I have often reflected, "Could more realistic prewar exercises have alleviated some of this loss?" I doubt it. The very nature of a torpedo attack in battle so preoccupies the crew that they are defenseless against unopposed fighters.

---

[*] From 4 to 6 June 1942, U.S. and Japanese naval forces fought a battle northwest of Midway Island in the Pacific. After Japanese bombers had struck the island, carrier-based U.S. dive-bombers attacked and sank the Japanese carriers. Torpedo Squadron Eight (VT-8), flying from the carrier Hornet (CV-8), was slaughtered by Japanese fighters while making its attack. Of 30 air crewmen in 15 TBDs, the only survivor was Ensign George H. Gay, USNR.

Q: The submariners also used an "is-was." As I understand, it was a circular slide rule, essentially.

Captain Merrill: Yes, that might have been functionally the same.

Q: Although you're dealing with faster approach speeds than a submarine would have.

Captain Merrill: Oh, definitely.

Q: Well, one thing, a point that was made about the TBD later was the vulnerability while it made that straight, level approach to the target, especially in the Battle of Midway.

Captain Merrill: We didn't realize how vulnerable we were. You're down there low, dedicated to a mission that you can't evade. We did have a tail gunner, as you know, but tail guns are not too effective. In the Battle of Midway I now believe that the plane that I flew routinely in VT-3 was the same as the VT-8 plane Ensign Gay ditched after being shot down.* He was picked up by a submarine and died only recently.

Q: That's fascinating.

Captain Merrill: Yes, I think so too. The plane was number 18 in both squadrons. I can't prove it, but that is a feeling I have.

Q: Well, please tell about shipboard life in an aircraft carrier. You had been in ship's company in the destroyers and the battleship. Now you were attached to the ship but not part of her crew.

---

* George Gay later wrote a memoir about his experiences, Sole Survivor: the Battle of Midway and its Effect on His Life (Naples, Florida: Naples Ad/Graphics Services, 1979).

Captain Merrill: Right, which, of course, means that a good fraction of the time--probably the majority of my time--was spent at an air station. From it you do your training, especially when the ship has to go into dry dock or deploy away. So you're really a visitor when you're an aviator assigned to the ship. But when you do come aboard, you get a pretty decent stateroom. Compared to destroyers, they were magnificent, and the mess was good. It was a well-run, comfortable ship, The Saratoga, just judging from my point of view, was also a well-commanded ship. I can't remember who the skipper was, frankly.

Q: Well, she was a newer ship than any that you had been on up to then.*

Captain Merrill: Right. A good ship that served the Navy well.

Q: Was there any friction between the black shoes and the brown shoes?†

Captain Merrill: No, I was never aware of that. They both had a job to do, and they were partners in making a weapons system go. They all knew that.

Q: Did your life center mostly around the squadron ready room when you were on board?

Captain Merrill: Yes, I would say so. When we were on board, there were plans for upcoming exercises to make. If nothing else, we had to do some brain work, study and so on. So we were busy, and that's the way it should be. There wasn't much idle chatter where

---

* The USS Saratoga (CV-3) was commissioned 16 November 1927. She had a standard displacement of 33,000 tons, was 888 feet long, 106 feet in the beam, an extreme width of 130 feet on the flight deck, and had a draft of 24 feet. She had a top speed of 33.5 knots and could accommodate approximately 60-70 aircraft. She was originally armed with eight 8-inch guns that were later removed in World War II.
† In the early days of naval aviation, the aviators wore brown shoes with their khaki uniforms and green uniforms. They thus acquired the nickname "brown shoes" to distinguish them from the traditional surface ship officers, who were known as "black shoes."

you were hanging around in the wardroom. There wasn't any television either, for that matter. [Laughter]

Q: Well, the ready room was kind of a sanctuary for the squadron.

Captain Merrill: Yes, it was. You could go there if you wanted to have a conversation with colleagues or whatever you wanted to do, or you could wander around the ship. But most of the time, you were doing some kind of a duty assignment.

Q: Did you have collateral duties?

Captain Merrill: Not in the sense that you would be a mess officer or something like that. You were still an aviator, and you were dedicated to be the best aviator you could be, including book learning, if necessary.

Q: What sorts of things were you studying in those books?

Captain Merrill: I can remember studies of tactics. There were manuals on air tactics and warfare that we had to know. Then there were technologies. For example, we had to keep our radio code skills up, which we all thought was useless. The need for code radio operations languished after voice radio came in. Backup code transmission was possible by keying the voice microphone. Both radios failed regularly because of vacuum tubes.

Q: So you mastered the skill of sending code at the same time you were flying your plane.

Captain Merrill: Yes, including reading it. You had to, because you might get caught in a situation where your life depended upon it.

Q: What do you remember about the maintenance of the aircraft?

Captain Merrill: That was a department that I didn't get directly involved in. There was, of course, a maintenance officer in the squadron, and he had a fleet of mechanics and technicians that took care of that. I wasn't involved in the operation, per se, but I certainly was interested in the efficiency with which they did their job. Generally speaking, I think a good job was done. There would be particular things, like this episode of fueling my tank and forgetting to put the cap back on. That was the worst experience I had, either from a maintenance or operational point of view.

Q: Well, I'll bet that never happened again to your plane.

Captain Merrill: Correct. But one of the things with the TBDs that we all feared was failing to lock the folding wings down before taking off. I mentioned this friend, Lester Stone, with whom we shared an apartment during flight training. He did that off of an air station runway in San Diego. He took off without locking his extended wings. He got flying speed up, the wings folded, and he crashed--barely surviving. As I remember it, there was a little red flag that stood up in the wing after extending, It was there to remind you to lock the wings by a separate crank. He missed that. Beware neglecting the pre-flight check-off list!

Q: Did you get involved in the ship's watch bill at all?

Captain Merrill: No, I don't think so. As I said, we aviators were visitors. It's hard to work officers with different professional agendas into a single watch list.

Q: What do you recall about your activities at the air station? Was that at North Island?

Captain Merrill: Yes, we were stationed on North Island. We had our own building, a hangar with adjoining offices. Usually it was good weather there, so the planes were parked on the apron outside of our hangar. When they had to have work done on them, they were brought in. Also, there was a huge establishment across the same field used for maintenance and overhaul of aircraft. So, if you had heavy maintenance to be done, you would just haul the airplane over there and get it done.

Q: Would you have an estimate of the proportion of time spent operating from the air station, compared with operating from the ship?

Captain Merrill: I'd say it was about two-thirds of the time on the air station, something like that. Two subjective factors favored the air station site, one was access to families and the other was to ease crowding on the ship.

Q: Was getting fuel a problem? Were operations curtailed for shortages?

Captain Merrill: No, none that I know of. At this point, the so-called Depression was "history," thanks to FDR. I don't remember fuel supply being something that curtailed our operations.

Q: Anything that you recall about aviation medicine during that period? I presume the physical was more strenuous that it had been previously.

Captain Merrill: Yes, once you got into aviation, the monitoring of your physical condition was pretty heavy. I think it was an annual physical that we had to go through. Of course, some people got caught up in that because the old body starts to degenerate. But fortunately I didn't have much trouble in that department.

Q: And I presume the heart murmur had just been a misdiagnosis?

Captain Merrill: It was. It proved to be a misdiagnosis by a nervous Nellie doctor.

Q: What do you recall of your family life during that period?

Captain Merrill: It was great. We had a house in Coronado, which was on the same island as the air station. We had friends around all over the place, so we had a great social life there. Mary Elizabeth's family was still living in Escondido nearby, so we'd drive up there frequently. There was plenty of entertainment and outdoor activities. I did a lot of fishing, especially off the Mexican coast.

Q: Was the pay sufficient to support a reasonable life-style?

Captain Merrill: Yes. As a matter of fact, we had a Mexican servant girl. We were relatively wealthy, because dollars, though few, bought a lot in those post-Depression days.

Q: Plus you had flight pay.

Captain Merrill: Yes, we had flight pay. So we didn't suffer. We didn't have very expensive needs. We had free public schools for the children when they came along. It was a good life.

Q: Did you get involved in any battle problems or fleet exercises in the Saratoga?

Captain Merrill: Indeed, I did. One that comes to mind was a mock attack on Pearl Harbor. We were flying the TBDs at this time, the year 1937. Saratoga was assigned to one of two opposing battle groups. Her air group made an attack on Pearl Harbor, not on Sunday, but otherwise almost like the Japs did later in 1941. Like the Japs, we approached out of the northwest quadrant. We flew southeast, made landfall on Oahu, and made a mock attack on Pearl Harbor. But we didn't go diving down and all those good things. We just flew symbolically over it.

That was only about four years before the Japs hit. I've wondered since if a full-blown simulated attack, with media coverage, on the ships, aircraft and buildings might have alerted Americans as to what the Japs might do.

Q: And that's a big reason why it was so successful.

Captain Merrill: Exactly.

Q: Did you get ashore in Honolulu at that point?

Captain Merrill: Yes, I'm sure we did. We came in there during the war game I mentioned and had a few days of shore leave, the usual island tours and so forth. My family wasn't with me, of course. Actually, we got clear out to Midway on that cruise. I don't think we made a mock attack on it, but I remember sailing by it.

Q: I would guess that was farther west than the fleet usually ventured in those years.

Captain Merrill: Yes, we had to go about halfway out for the sake of the war game, so somebody decided let's go all the way out and see what Midway looks like.

Q: What did it look like?

Captain Merrill: Just another flat atoll. There wasn't much on it. From a deep draft ship we couldn't see the details.

Q: Did you have any other unusual experiences comparable to the missing gas cap?

Captain Merrill: Well, I can remember one other operation that unnerved me. TorpRon 3 was given a mission to do a scouting search. The idea was to find an enemy ship or encounter their aircraft. The tactic was to cover a sector by flying three legs, relative to one's (moving) carrier.

Q: Kind of a pie-shaped wedge.

Captain Merrill: Yes, like a pie-shaped wedge. So I was assigned to a certain sector. The weather conditions were not ideal by a long shot. There was a high overcast and a gusty wind blowing; we had to take all of that into account to do our own navigation. On top of everything else, we had to maintain radio silence unless we had a dangerous emergency. This meant we could not update our navigation. We had to have the right plot when we left, or any contact reports would be in error and we might miss the ship upon return.

I flew my pattern that way. At five minutes minus rendezvous, I started looking hard for Saratoga. Visibility had decreased and when it came time for the intercept, no Saratoga. Training kicked in. When a contact is lost, one's doctrine is to fly a "retiring search curve," which I'm sure you're familiar with that. So I started that, and about ten minutes later saw the ship--just before deciding to break radio silence.

Q: So there was no electronic signal from the ship, at that point, to home on.

Captain Merrill: Correct. I don't know whether the ship ever changed course or speed. I don't think so. I think it was just natural variations in the wind probably, and maybe my airspeed was off or whatever. Anyway, everybody got home. It's just that I personally became acquainted with that well-known phrase, "The lonely sea."

Q: Were there occasions when the whole air group operated together?

Captain Merrill: Oh, yes, but usually at air shows. We'd fly parades for the general public, for example over San Diego. That involved some tricky tactics just to form up on time and all that. Then, of course, there were air group attacks on "enemy" battle lines. The dominant concept of naval power in action was battleships versus battleships; air groups were seen only as adjuncts to the inevitable heavy gun duel between battle lines. We should have been simulating Midway instead of Jutland.[*]

---

[*] The Battle of Jutland was a classic encounter between British and German battleships in May 1916.

Q: Right.

Captain Merrill: Generally speaking, our attacks were pretty well coordinated. We'd come in and make a mock torpedo attack, but all we would actually do is fly low over the water in the general direction of a column of battleships.

Q: Well, and you'd like to be covered by the fighters so you get some protection as you make that approach.

Captain Merrill: Yes, the fighters were stationed at points where they could give you cover. It was all great, but, as it came out at Midway, sometimes the best laid plans of mice and men go awry. The fighters weren't there, and all the torpedo planes were shot down.

Q: You talk about these displays for the public. There was a real glamour to aviation in that era.

Captain Merrill: Yes. Such displays had the function of alerting the populace--making them conscious that they had a Navy, including these airplanes. You have to have public support to keep a defense system viable; their tax dollars are paying for it.

Q: Well, in that era, very few people would have a chance to travel by airplane, which is commonplace now. So it would be much more exciting, I would think.

Captain Merrill: Oh, yes.

Q: Less taken for granted.

Captain Merrill: That's right.

Q: As the '30s moved along and Japan was becoming more and more of a threat, did you get intelligence on the Japanese?

Captain Merrill: If you mean the U.S. Navy, I don't know.

Q: Well, at your level.

Captain Merrill: At my level, I'd say no. I'd say what we learned about the Japanese Navy we got from the movies and read in the newspaper. I can't remember any regular publications or briefings coming out to us that said, "Well, now, here's what we know about the Japanese Navy." It wasn't focused, even though we knew that Japan was the probable enemy. Whatever intelligence came was dispersed at the top level, and that's where it stayed. There was a great preoccupation with broad-based security, which I think was a giant anchor on the Navy more than an obstacle for Japanese spies.

Q: What manifestations did you see of that preoccupation?

Captain Merrill: Well, in terms of broad-based security, there was a definite tendency, I think, to over-classify documents. We had a structure in those days that made "confidential" the highest I ever saw; "secret" was the kind of thing that you wouldn't even tell your wife about. [Laughter]

This made it hard to get access to the things that you needed to know. Security over-classification persisted during and after World War II. I was reading in one of your oral histories about Carleton Shugg, then CEO at Electric Boat.* He told a story of having to go on a flight to San Diego or someplace in California while carrying a "top secret" briefcase with some numbers and data in it. He got to an intermediate airport where a security agent interviewed him and found out that he was transporting this top secret

---

* Shugg's recollections are contained in the Naval Institute's oral history volume on the Polaris program.

briefcase. The agent said, "You've got to have a security guard. Either you wear a gun or you take a security guard with you."

Shugg refused to carry a gun, so he was assigned a security guard. The pair flew on, stopping at another city, where they had some lunch. Here both Shugg and the agent forgot his padlocked briefcase and got on the plane in time for takeoff. When airborne the agent suddenly said, "My God, where is the briefcase?" Of course, it was back there in the lunchroom. [Laughter]

So they turned the airplane around, landed, retrieved the padlocked briefcase and resumed the flight. You can imagine the mood of the crew and passengers at this point!

Q: Well, did that concern, preoccupation with security, produce frustrations for you specifically?

Captain Merrill: Not to the point where I made any protests about it. My personal conviction was that it was too much at this particular point in time. And I got even more convinced of it as I got higher responsibilities, as at Point Mugu and the Special Projects Office.

Q: Were there things that you thought you should know that were denied to you?

Captain Merrill: Well, we spoke of one of them right there. After each war game I was unconvinced that these games adequately simulated an actual war situation. In actuality, each war situation is set up and played out not only by you, but by the enemy as well. So if we were getting intelligence about the Japanese, it never appeared in these games, at least to the best of my knowledge. I do not remember participating in an organized critique of a war game, nor did I ever read such a critique, which of course would be classified. As junior officers we were considered too lacking in experience to contribute.

Q: Well, in Admiral Jimmy Thach's oral history, he talks about getting intelligence out of China, where the Chinese and Japanese were at war.* And what he was able to deduce about the capabilities of the Zero led him to develop the Thach Weave to counter the Zero.

Captain Merrill: Great.

Q: Fortunately some of it was getting through.

Captain Merrill: Well, I think that's great. Of course, that was his job, or was it? Where was he when he developed that?

Q: He was commanding officer of VF-3.

Captain Merrill: Well, I've got to commend him. He probably had to go dig it out, despite his rank and command status. I think the intelligence probably didn't get to him on a routine basis.

Q: That may well be. Anything else about that tour in the torpedo squadron to remember?

Captain Merrill: No. We've touched on what memories I have of it and some of the things that happened to it later.

Q: You mentioned going to PG school, and typically that was something that an officer got to after about seven years of sea duty.

Captain Merrill: Well, let's see. I came to Annapolis to go to the PG school in the summer of 1941. That was seven years after graduation and on track career-wise.

    About December 10, 1941, I was out flying over the Chesapeake Bay in a seaplane, keeping up my flight skills. I was still digesting the news of Pearl Harbor. Certainly one of

---

* The oral history of Admiral John S. Thach, USN (Ret.), is in the Naval Institute collection.

the things I thought of was whether they would discontinue the PG school and bring all the pilots back because they needed them. I was prepared and expected to have that happen. But it didn't.

Even after Pearl Harbor, we went on with the PG course, but it was foreshortened. It used to be a two-year program, leading to a master's degree, but they foreshortened it. Fortunately, they had the wisdom to stop the operation in Annapolis, which was book-oriented, and get us up to MIT, which was hardware oriented.[*] We learned an awful lot up there, because we saw things that were in development there that we hadn't any notion of, things on the leading edge of technology.

Q: What would be examples?

Captain Merrill: One example would be radar. We didn't know about radar, even though its first development was at the Naval Research Laboratory--another example of over-zealous security. Another was the magnetron, coming in as part of the radar program. We aviators recognized it as the key to later airborne radars.

We also learned about embryonic work in digital computers. I remember being taken to the University of Pennsylvania to see the Univac. It was housed in a huge room, hotter than Billy be Damned, because of the thousands of vacuum tubes in there. The mean time before failure, they told us, was something like three hours, and then the whole computer would go down again. Later on, of course, it was compared to a modern personal computer like the one we're looking at right now. Functionally this is equal to or better than the Univac in computing power. So MIT was a revelation, not only as to what was shown to us but also as to the potential for applications based on the state of the art.

Q: What was the curriculum of study in Annapolis?

Captain Merrill: It was straight electrical engineering, dominated by power transmission. The most sophisticated equipment that I remember working on in Annapolis was a volt

---

[*] MIT--Massachusetts Institute of Technology.

ohmmeter. We did have one oscilloscope so we could see wave forms. But we had plenty of volt ohmmeters, and I remember working on circuits, measuring resistance and current and proving that the multiplication of volts and amps equals watts of power. It was simple stuff, and our textbooks were pretty elementary. The whole state of the art was elementary at that point. I also remember being taken over to the naval radio towers here in Annapolis. We were a class of some ten young officers, eager to learn about this worldwide radio transmission system, the Navy's best.

Q: These are the radio antennas that you can still see at Greenbury Point.

Captain Merrill: Yes. We went over there to see what was going on. Of course, they were using code to contact ships all over the world. We came into a room where there was a large group of enlisted men, seated in rows up and down a long bench. They were transmitting in code, sending messages. When they sent these messages, they could hear their transmissions in their earphones, actually the signals as they went out. This helped them speed up everything and minimize mistakes. That was all explained to us, as well as where the messages were going to and at what frequency.

That done, we all crowded around one salty old chief. He was busy doing his thing until suddenly he reached up, took his headphones off, set them down, and nonchalantly continued to send code. We instinctively recognized that he was pulling something on us, and so I said, "Well, what's going on here, Chief?"

He replied, "Well, I hate to tell you this, but I got a gold filling in a tooth here and that's a detector. So I hear the signal whether I have the earphones on or not." [Laughter]

Q: So he wasn't pulling your leg?

Captain Merrill: No. His tooth was acting like a semi-conductor detector. The radio field under the towers was so powerful he could hear it in his ear.

Q: How challenging was that curriculum compared with studying electrical engineering when you were a midshipman?

Captain Merrill: It was just an extension of it. They could have covered electric motors, solenoids, switches etc. but it would not have been useful to us. Of course, the course was cut short by the onset of war.

Q: In retrospect, how capable were the instructors in the PG school?

Captain Merrill: I remember one professor whose name was Giet. He was our top professor, and we had a great deal of affection for him. He was down to earth. He taught us as he found us. He took the capabilities that we had and focused them. He taught us right up to those capabilities. But we also had a rather scatter-brained doctor, whose name I don't remember. He would give us lectures on differential equations as applied to transients in a circuit and stuff like that. At best we studied mathematics, with a vague relationship to electrical engineering. We had a great mathematician up there, but he was intent on impressing us with his knowledge. He'd get up at the blackboard, and a whole hour would go by. At the bell we'd have all these equations up there and depart half asleep. But Giet was just the opposite. He's probably deceased now.

Q: So are you suggesting that you weren't stretched too much by that experience?

Captain Merrill: Yes. But as soon as we got up to MIT, we were stretched, fascinated, and challenged.

Q: What do you recall about your family life in Annapolis then?

Captain Merrill: Well, we had a family tragedy here. My second son, Hugh, was born in the naval hospital here. We lived over on Weems Creek in a rented apartment. I was going to PG School. One day my wife put him down on a crib mattress on top of a regular bed.

The mattress had one of these covers where you tied a collar around the child's neck and then tucked the cover around underneath the mattress. Against all odds, he managed to scrunch around out from under the cover and hung himself on the collar. I found him hanging there when I returned from work. It was too late for resuscitation.

Q: How old was he at the time?

Captain Merrill: He was about nine months old. He's buried in the Naval Academy cemetery along with his mother, who died after we were married 42 years. Hugh's death was a tragedy that often happens in families. We survived it all right.

Q: You said that it was more useful for you to take the PG in electrical engineering rather than aeronautical. Why do you say that?

Captain Merrill: Because the technology of electronics rapidly displaced electrical engineering and had even more impact on naval aviation than did aeronautical engineering. I'll rephrase it this way. Through the latter, airplanes became faster, longer in range, and better platforms for people and payloads. But electronics enabled them to fly and navigate in bad weather, pin-point targets and destroy them with accurate guided missiles. Electronics were essential to guided missiles and drove my career into that specialty. That's why, in retrospect, I'm glad I studied electrical rather than aeronautical engineering.

Q: When you were at MIT, did you have any contact with Dr. Stark Draper?*

Captain Merrill: I sure did.

Q: What do you recall about him.?

---

* Dr. Stark Draper of the Massachusetts Institute of Technology had an important role in the development of the inertial navigation systems used in Polaris missiles and later in the space missions sent to the moon.

Captain Merrill: As a person he was downright brilliant. He was a chain-smoker, as I remember it. But he was also a great innovator. I credit him as the "father of inertial guidance," for example. He also played a part in airborne radar development. But I'm most familiar with his work in inertial guidance. In the mid-'50s I worked with him as technical director of the Polaris ballistic missile development program. We went to him for the prototype of the missile's inertial guidance.

Q: I've gathered that he had a down-to-earth personality.

Captain Merrill: Very much so. He was very practical. He cussed now and then to turn off rhetorical bores, but most people loved the guy. The various graduate students that worked for him almost worshipped him. He had this Stark Draper Laboratory that was gradually developed and named for him. There is no doubt about it, he was one of the technical leaders of his time.

Q: Anything else you remember about the period we've covered this morning to add on?

Captain Merrill: No. I'm sure that I'll think of some things, but we can take care of that when the time comes. I'd say this is probably a logical break point, because it's really the point at which my career branched off into guided missiles. Heretofore I had no suspicion of this.

Q: Well, we're off to an excellent start. I thank you very much.

Captain Merrill: Well, thank you. I'm looking forward to the next session.

Interview Number 2 with Captain Grayson Merrill, U.S. Navy (Retired)

Place: Captain Merrill's home, Annapolis, Maryland

Date: Thursday, 7 November 1996

Interviewer: Paul Stillwell

Q: Well, Captain, it's great to see you again on a beautiful fall day.

Captain Merrill: Right.

Q: When we finished last time, you had been talking about your experience in postgraduate school. Then your career was ready to break off and lead toward the guided missile field. So if you could resume there, please.

Captain Merrill: Okay. Then-Commander Delmar Fahrney and I had come into casual contact at various places, including Guantanamo, Cuba.* So I was somewhat aware of what he was doing in the field of radio-controlled aircraft. In spite of that, I was quite surprised--when I came toward the end of my postgraduate course--to receive orders assigning me to the Bureau of Aeronautics, working for him in the Special Design Branch. As I learned more about where I was going, I got more and more excited about it. I realized that this field was the cradle of guided missiles in the Navy, at least in the Bureau of Aeronautics.†

Q: Well, you didn't really have that realization at the time, did you?

---

* Commander Delmar S. Fahrney, USN.
† For an excellent history of the subject, see Rear Admiral Delmar S. Fahrney, USN (Ret.), "The Birth of Guided Missiles," U.S. Naval Institute Proceedings, December 1980, pages 54-60.

Captain Merrill: I did, but in a limited sort of way. I talked to people who knew Del Fahrney and what he was doing. In the process I learned about the assault drone program, clearly the Navy's first guided missile.

Q: I see, so there was already the notion then of making it into a weapon.

Captain Merrill: Oh, yes. The assault drone program was in place before I came to the Special Design Branch, so I realized that.

In a very short space of time, I moved my family down to Falls Church, Virginia, and reported for duty. I don't know exactly when, but I guess it would be in late fall of 1942. I soon got a feel for the scope of the work that was going on.

Q: How large was the group?

Captain Merrill: The group consisted of the assault drone officers, perhaps three or four of those. Then there was another group that supported the "glomb" (glider bomb) program. That, again, consisted of three officers, because it was a large program at that particular point. Then there were the smaller programs, the experimental programs, if you will, such as Gorgon.*

Q: Was there still a target drone section?†

Captain Merrill: Oh, yes. That was quite strong. So, all in all, I would guess we had something like 20 officers, plus the clerical people.

I might mention in passing that one of the two clerical people was a yeoman first class whose name was Melanie Holmes. She was very competent, and there was a second

---

* The Gorgon program, 1946-51, was a generic missile development program that had multiple configurations, based on alternate airframes, propulsion, and guidance. It could be launched from either air or ground.
† As Fahrney's article relates, the assault drones were developed from the radio-controlled drones that were used for antiaircraft gunnery practice by U.S. Navy ships.

yeoman named Jo Anderson. Amazingly, after I left the Special Design Branch, Melanie Holmes went on in the Naval Reserve to become a full captain. When she learned that I was going to participate in the 50th anniversary celebration of the Pacific Missile Test Range at Point Mugu, she wrote me a letter. We later got reacquainted out there in October 1996.

Q: Were those two women in the WAVES back in '42?[*]

Captain Merrill: Indeed they were.

Q: They must have been among the very earliest.

Captain Merrill: They were. I don't know who detailed them to the office, but I'm grateful for it. I think Melanie was a yeoman first class. Later she accompanied the site survey board on the trip that selected the Point Mugu location.[†] She was the stenographer/historian for the board.

Q: Where was the headquarters of the facility that was running these programs?

Captain Merrill: The entire Bureau of Aeronautics was in a claptrap "temporary" building on Constitution Avenue in Washington. It's since been totally replaced, of course, but that's where it was.

Q: I think the Vietnam War Veterans Memorial is there now, in that vicinity.

Captain Merrill: Yes, probably so.

---

[*] WAVES--Women accepted for Voluntary Emergency Service.
[†] As he related later in the oral history, Captain Merrill was instrumental in the establishment of the Naval Air Missile Test Center at Point Mugu, California, in 1946.

Q: Well, you can't do any flying on the mall in Washington. Where were the aircraft?

Captain Merrill: The pioneering place where flight operations were going on was the Naval Aircraft Factory in Philadelphia, which later expanded to the Naval Air Material Center. Captain Fahrney was assigned there after he came back from the Pacific.

The Philadelphia organization had a life of its own, which goes back many years.[*] That's where most of the early 1930s target drone development went on. Fahrney turned naturally to them, because they knew how to build airplanes. The early Gorgon missiles, for example, were built up there. The radio controls, autopilots, etc., for target drones were mostly improvised by talented utility squadron enlisted ratings who were soon promoted to officers after the war broke out.

Q: Was that the Navy counterpart of the Army's facility at Wright Field in Dayton, Ohio?

Captain Merrill: Yes, except the Army had its management headquarters there, as well as actual development. In our case, the headquarters of the Special Design Branch was in Washington. And that was true also of our "friendly competitors," the Bureau of Ordnance.

Q: Was it more difficult to have the headquarters separated from where the air operations were?

Captain Merrill: No, I don't think so. Maybe it was a blessing in disguise, as a matter of fact, because the focus of the Special Design Branch was managing the various programs. We had a lot of traffic back and forth with contractors, as well as the Naval Aircraft Factory.

We were a "class desk" of BuAer, thus ranking "with but after" other class desks such as fighters, patrol planes, etc.[†] We dealt mostly with the electronics division, as you

---
[*] See William F. Trimble, Wings for the Navy: A History of the Naval Aircraft Factory, 1917-1956 (Annapolis: Naval Institute Press, 1990).
[†] BuAer--Bureau of Aeronautics.

can imagine, but also with all of the other functional divisions, especially the production division in the case of assault drones.

At one time there were some 1,500 of these assault drones on order, and as their popularity in the program lessened, so did the number on order. The final number probably was more like 200. Not surprisingly, many officers in BuAer resented any diverting of effort from war planes to untried guided missiles. Schedule slippages of assault drone production clearly contributed to periodic downsizing within the program. A typical handicap to schedules was a well-intentioned edict that the assault drones and glombs had to use wood for their structures

Q: Was Fahrney in charge of all these separate elements you've enumerated with the drones, the glide bombs, and the targets?

Captain Merrill: He directed them, yes. And it was an interesting thing, historically speaking, that the glomb program grew out of the relationship between Fahrney and Commander Ralph Barnaby, who was at the Naval Aircraft Factory.*

Q: And he had a strong background in gliders.

Captain Merrill: Right. You probably know about that. He had strong ties to the DuPont family in Delaware. The officer in charge of the glomb program, if I remember correctly, either was a DuPont or very closely tied to them, a very able young man.

Q: I'd be interested in your recollections of Fahrney and Barnaby, both in terms of management style and leadership and personality.

Captain Merrill: All right. I regarded Fahrney primarily as sort of a visionary. He was strong in visualizing what could be done with the technology that he was familiar with. So

---

* Commander Ralph S. Barnaby, USN. The oral history of Barnaby, who retired as a captain, is in the Naval Institute collection.

he probably was the first officer in the Navy--in company with Bobby Jones, as we called him--who conceived the assault drone program.* You asked about his management style. Fahrney was a big, jovial person, very well informed technically because of his background and postgraduate training. Not so much in electronics as he was in aeronautics. Electronics skills were pretty thin at that time in the Navy.

As I mentioned before, I originally sought to specialize as an aeronautical engineer but wound up in electronics, one of the best things that ever happened to me. Anyhow, we complemented each other in our technical backgrounds. Del Fahrney was one who developed contacts outside of the office, more than I did. He had friendships with Major Holloman in the Air Force, for example, and also with Dundas Tucker, who was then in the Bureau of Ordnance.†

Dundas Tucker was a counterpart in the Bureau of Ordnance to Fahrney in the Bureau of Aeronautics. Fortunately, they were good friends, and they saw to it that turf wars didn't enter into their work. We enjoyed a lot of cooperation from the Bureau of Ordnance and they from us. I could name a number of examples, but the important thing is Fahrney and his ability to get cooperation from the Air Force and the Bureau of Ordnance.

Del related similarly to Ralph Barnaby up at the Naval Aircraft Factory. They were close personal friends. Barnaby was also jovial, outgoing, and laid back. He was not a workaholic, by any means. Neither was Fahrney, for that matter. I found myself complementing Fahrney in that respect. He would have the visions, and I would put them down on paper so that they got done. I was pretty good on following up on whether things were being done.

Q: Would you describe yourself as a workaholic?

Captain Merrill: I'd pretty well have to, I guess.

---

* Lieutenant Robert F. Jones, USN.
† Major George V. Holloman, USA. Holloman subsequently died in a B-17 accident on Formosa in 1946; in 1948 Holloman Air Force Base, New Mexico, was named in his honor. Lieutenant Commander Dundas P. Tucker, USN. The official name at the time was the U.S. Army Air Forces; in 1947 it split off from the Army and became the U.S. Air Force.

Q: What kind of hours did you keep during the war?

Captain Merrill: Theoretically, we worked an eight-hour day. In actuality, I tended to get there at least on time, if not early in the office, and seldom got home before 6:00 o'clock in the evening. Of course, I did a lot of traveling, which was necessary. I must admit that I drifted into full workaholic mode later on, especially in the Polaris program. Both of us felt the pressure of the assault drone program.

By the time I got there, the development of the TDR-1 was pretty well in hand. It had been redesigned by the Interstate Aircraft Company from what the Naval Aircraft Factory (NAF) did with the TDN-1.[*] NAF received an order for 100 TDN-1s.[†] They were seen as a pilot program for the Interstate Aircraft production as well as an initial allotment to the Special Air Task Force (SATFOR).

To sum up, I had great admiration for Del Fahrney and so did everybody that worked in the Special Design Branch. They worked liked tigers in there, both for him and me.

Q: What was his vision in 1942? What did he hope to achieve during the war?

Captain Merrill: Originally, as the formulator of the assault drone program, he envisaged an orderly, progressive program for producing a pilot quantity for test and evaluation, followed by production to support training in newly created squadrons and then deployment to the Pacific for attacks from aircraft carriers. What actually happened was that Bobby Jones teamed up with Captain Oscar Smith to sell CominCh, then Admiral King on getting these assault drones out as quickly as possible into the fleet.[‡] They believed that we had a

---

[*] TDN-1 was the designation of the Naval Aircraft Factory's assault drone. TDR-1 was the Interstate designation for the same aircraft.
[†] This order was placed by BuAer in March 1942 for delivery in November of that year. For details, see chapter 12, "Assault Drones, Glombs, and Guided Missiles," pages 258-287 of Trimble's book on the Naval Aircraft Factory.
[‡] Captain Oscar Smith, USN, was on the staff of the Chief of Naval Operations in Washington; he was promoted to commodore as of April 1943. Admiral Ernest J. King,

superb surprise weapon, capable of wiping out part of the Japanese fleet. In actual fact, they didn't get into action until toward the end of the war. By then the Japs had few ships left, so the drones were expended against island AA defenses.*

Q: It's interesting, because Oscar Smith was not an aviator; he was a surface officer. How did he become involved in this?

Captain Merrill: He didn't pay any attention as to whether he was an aviator or not. What he did feel, in his gut, was that this was the coming type of weapon the Navy ought to have, and he was right. But it was troubling to other people that he was not an aviator. I personally don't believe that being an aviator had very much to do with his competence. He was a hard-driving, brilliant person, and he believed in the weapon that he was trying to sell. And sell it he did. He was also close to Admiral King, who eventually bought it--lock, stock, and barrel. It was King's endorsement of the assault drone program that started the ball rolling and kept it so, despite its lack of test, evaluation and trained operators and its potential to interfere with the massive offense then in place to defeat Japan.

Q: What was the guidance mechanism at that point, in 1942? How did you get it from wherever it started to the target?

Captain Merrill: The earliest target drone system was created by of a group of talented enlisted technicians and pilots who were recruited by Bobby Jones into his utility squadron based at NAS Cape May and the Naval Aircraft Factory.† Their task was to convert several simple aircraft to radio control targets. Naturally, they turned to existing equipments that they knew about. The first example was the autopilot. The Sperry autopilot was the basic

---

USN, served as Chief of Naval Operations from 26 March 1942 to 15 December 1945 and as Commander in Chief U.S. Fleet (CominCh) from 20 December 1941 to 2 September 1945; he was promoted to the rank of fleet admiral in December 1944.
* AA--antiaircraft.
† Jones commanded VJ-5, Utility Squadron Five, based at Naval Air Station Cape May, New Jersey.

element that existed at that point. But it was just an autopilot that people could turn on once they were in the air. They needed to fly the drone off and back onto an airstrip and do it by radio control. The second basic element was a voice radio system, probably at VHF frequency.* Anyway, they modified these elements and linked them into a system that worked.

Q: Well, was this the same technology that was used in the target drones?

Captain Merrill: The target drone technology had to be augmented to do the assault drone job. In order precisely to hit a target, TV guidance had to be added. RCA was contracted to develop an airborne camera/transmitter and a control plane receiver/display.† This they did under the supervision of the Naval Research Laboratory. Concurrently, the TDN and TDR assault drones were being designed to carry either a bomb or torpedo as well as disposable landing gear to be jettisoned after takeoff.

Several flight tests were then staged in and near Cape May, during which a drone crashed into a billboard target on Bloodsworth Island.‡ This was enough to trigger Admiral King to order some 1,500 assault drones and creation of a three-squadron force to train and deploy to the fleet.

I personally knew about these tests only by hearsay, but their primitive design and analyses, compared to the sales impact, haunted me for the remainder of the war. The episode was a strong motive for my advocacy of a postwar missile test range for the Navy.

Q: Right.

Captain Merrill: In the interests of history I would like to recite the story of Admiral King and the British Navy's Bumblebee.

---

* VHF--very high frequency.
† RCA--Radio Corporation of America.
‡ Bloodsworth Island is in the Chesapeake Bay, near Dorchester County, Maryland.

Apparently the British early on recognized the value of an AA radio-controlled target drone, possibly because they were at war and we weren't. Anyhow, a demonstration was made to Admiral King of their "Bumblebee" target. He was most impressed, particularly with the corrective action which ensued within their gunnery fraternity.

On his return the admiral told Fahrney to get busy and contact the British and use their Bumblebee technology as much as he could. In the meantime, our own little crew under Bobby Jones, and Barnaby at the Naval Aircraft Factory, were going ahead using our equipment. So it was not necessary to copy what the British did but simply to use what we already had, which was the equivalent. They soon had these target drones flying, for example, down in Guantanamo. They flew a lot of exercises with the fleet, thus stimulating some very sharp reviews of antiaircraft fire in our Navy.

Q: So it was back in the '30s that King had viewed the Bumblebee?

Captain Merrill: Yes, but in the late '30s[*]

Q: How did the radio signals run the control surfaces on the drone?

Captain Merrill: A simple answer is, "Quite like your TV controller at home." Once the TV is plugged in, the radio receiver can detect a tone which switches the TV to "On." Thereafter you can change channels, volume, etc. The following description of the drone control system may well be inaccurate, owing to my fading memory, but it is essentially correct.

In the drone control system a pilot in a ground cart or cockpit of a "chase" plane used a modified VHF voice transmitter to send commands to a matched receiver in the drone. He had a "joy stick" which emulated regular aircraft controls--push forward to nose the drone down, pull back to nose it up and so on. Each drone had normal pilot-powered wire controls for manned flight. But for "nolo" flight, electric motors controlled from the

---

[*] Vice Admiral Ernest J. King, USN, served as Commander Aircraft Battle Force from January 1938 to June 1939.

VHF receiver actuated the ailerons, elevator, rudder, throttle, bomb/torpedo arming, torpedo release, TV on/off switch, autopilot on/off switch, etc.

Modifications were needed to the VHF transmitter to modulate it, not with voice but with audio tones--one distinct tone for each command. The receiver had to have a multiple tone filter to decipher the commands coming in.

As the program went on, various improvements were made. For example, a new autopilot, using optical versus mechanical pickoffs, was independently developed.

Takeoffs were made by a skilled pilot sitting in a Jeep-type vehicle, usually with a copilot by his side. In a similar way, they also did the landings. The vehicles could be taken aboard a carrier for drone operations. Once the drone was safely airborne, a waiting chase plane would fly formation on the drone and take over its control. For a gunnery exercise the chase plane would line up the drone on the desired course and then back away to a safe position. Once the exercise was over, the chase plane would bring it back to ground control for a landing. Realistic maneuvers were common during firing runs and the inability of 5- and 3-inch guns to cope with them awakened the Navy to the vulnerability of its ships to air attacks.

An assault drone mission from a carrier against an enemy ship was similar but more complex. The takeoff had to deal with roll and pitch on deck; remote control will never be a match for pilot control in this situation. Also, landing gear had to be jettisoned, TV turned on, payload armed, and, finally, the target accurately hit. I'm unsure whether it was ever done with the production drones.

Q: What would be the difference in the way you would control an assault drone and a glide bomb?

Captain Merrill: The main difference was that the glide bomb would be towed by a control plane to the vicinity of the target at a fairly high altitude. The same plane could both tow and control, The pilot would position his plane where he was sure he had enough glide distance to make the attack, hopefully with the target already on his TV display. Then he'd release the glomb into a glide path, under autopilot control. At this point he was free to maneuver out of any danger from defensive surface gunfire. After arming the bomb, the controller used radio and the TV image to guide the glomb into the target.

There were some very interesting variations on that, which are worth noting. Somebody got the idea, instead of towing the glomb off a runway, which is a time-consuming and intricate thing, especially if you're on a carrier, why not have the control plane "snatch" the glomb off the carrier's deck? The concept involved snaking down a stretchable plastic towline on the foredeck just ahead of the glomb. The forward end would be configured as a wide loop to be strung between two poles spanning the foredeck. A carrier-type airplane, with a modified tailhook, would then be flown so as to snatch the loop with the tailhook, absorb shock and energy by stretching the towline, and ending with the glomb airborne and under tow. It sounds like a Rube Goldberg invention, but the glider fraternity had done it off a Delaware runway with lighter commercial aircraft and were keen to do it off a carrier!*

Q: Was this a regular carrier tailhook that was used to pick it up?

Captain Merrill: No. Obviously that would have been an advantage, but the requirements were different. For example, releasing from a slack carrier arresting wire versus a taut towline.

Q: How long was the towline?

Captain Merrill: It would be around 500 feet.

Q: You'd have to have pretty precise flying to hook that thing, wouldn't you?

---

* Reuben L. "Rube" Goldberg (1883-1970) was a popular syndicated newspaper cartoonist best known for drawings of mechanical devices that used absurdly unnecessary complexity to achieve simple actions.

Captain Merrill: They actually practiced this on a field. I don't think they ever got on a carrier deck. They used a regular landing signals officer to help make the snatch.

Q: The Germans, of course, used some of those glide bombs in combat. Was our development essentially parallel to the Germans at that point?

Captain Merrill: The German HS-293 was functionally like our glombs except that it was visually guided and dropped from the wing of an aircraft. The time line for the two weapons was probably about the same, but the HS-293 sank some ships, starting in 1943. Incidentally, the Bureau of Ordnance was working on a radar homing glide bomb named Bat at about the same time. As you know, Dr. Herbert Wagner, an Austrian, worked for me at Point Mugu after the war. He developed the HS-293.

Q: Which they had a couple of spectacular successes with.

Captain Merrill: Yes, they did.

Q: They hit the cruiser Savannah and a troopship called the Rohna.*

Captain Merrill: I remember reading about that.

Q: What was your particular piece of this as it went along?

Captain Merrill: In the glomb work I was sort of an executive officer under Del Fahrney. But I worked through officers who had "class desk" responsibilities for each category of missile. It was a conventional organization, from a management point of view. I knew

---

* The German Henschel HS-293 severely damaged the U.S. light cruiser Savannah (CL-42) off Salerno, Sicily, on 11 September 1943 and destroyed the Italian battleship Roma on 9 September 1943. More than 1,000 American troops were killed on 26 November 1943 when a glide bomb sank the British troopship Rohna. See Carlton Jackson, Forgotten Tragedy: The Sinking of HMT Rohna (Annapolis: Naval Institute Press, 1996).

pretty much everything that was going on in the branch and participated in the major decisions. We even found time to think ahead a little.

Q: Well, that was Fahrney's job, as you've described it.

Captain Merrill: Well, yes, but we really did it together, I would say. We didn't have formal brainstorming sessions, you might say. If we were at lunch, we'd get to talking about some technology or operating concept, and the first thing you know we'd have an idea. If it was a good idea, we'd try to define a "next step." Maybe we'd want to talk to the Air Force about it, because they had already done it or whatever. Those things often came up out of nowhere.

Q: Was there any problem in getting the funding for these ideas?

Captain Merrill: Not really. I never felt that we suffered from lack of money. There was a lot of defensive talk about it, but my view was that whenever we got a concept in our heads that something should be done, even including the Navy missile sea test range, the next step was thinking it through thoroughly and putting it down on paper. If the result made sense, it usually got funded. My paper "Pilotless Aircraft for Fleet Use in 1950" was another such an idea.

Q: What other examples do you remember of those concepts that you pushed forward?

Captain Merrill: I think the Gorgon program was probably one example. We came up with the realization that in Gorgon we had an air-launched guided missile that we knew would fly reliably. We also had different concepts for advanced guidance devices, such as advanced television and homing radar for aircraft targets. We decided to use Gorgon as a general-purpose test vehicle. At low cost, we could try out new guidance components, learn about them "hands on," and even make demonstrations as proof of practicability. We then could ask for funding to design, develop, and test a "mil spec" missile.[*] I can't remember how many versions of Gorgon we had on the books, but I do recall that Sparrow I had a radar whose roots went back to Gorgon.[†] Actually, after the war, Gorgon was still useful as a test vehicle.

We had other concepts as well. In 1942 the Japs had plenty of ships, and we didn't, as a result of Pearl Harbor. So the thought was that we could quickly develop a weapon for the dive bomber people. The SBDs were the main aircraft that were doing this job.[‡] We prepared specs for an air-to-ground missile called Gargoyle. Essentially, it was a little JATO-propelled flying machine with a 1,000-pound bomb in it.[§] No television, simple radio control, and a 1,000-pound bomb. We added a smoke flare to give the pilot an aiming point.

The pilot's task was to get into a dive bombing position, similar to what they did later at Midway, and then fire the missile. Its JATO would get it ahead of the launch plane and flying faster. The pilot steered it into the target using a small joystick on top of his main stick. As it turned out, events outpaced the missile's development and test. I have a patent on it, and it is totally worthless. [Laughter]

The viewpoint of Navy decision-makers shifted markedly during the last year or so of the war, insofar as the guided missiles of that era were concerned. The whole scenario in the Pacific had turned around. We had won such battles as Coral Sea, Midway, Philippine Sea, and so forth. The Japs were on the defensive, and the attitude of the commanders in the fleet had changed. They weren't yelling for new weapons; they were yelling for more of what they already had because it was working. That's very understandable. Indeed, the

---

[*] Mil spec--military specifications.
[†] Since the late 1950s the Sparrow has been the U.S. Navy's major long-range air defense missile. The Sparrow I version entered fleet service in 1956 on board F3H Demons and F7U Cutlasses.
[‡] The Douglas-built SBD Dauntless, which entered fleet squadrons in 1941, was a most successful dive-bomber in the early part of World War II. It was instrumental in the sinking of four Japanese aircraft carriers in the Battle of Midway.
[§] JATO--jet-assisted takeoff, a means of giving a boost in speed and thrust to propeller-driven aircraft.

introduction of new weapons was just a diversion as far as they were concerned. This attitude prevailed toward the assault drones, even though they had already been deployed.

Q: Well, you could draw a parallel on the air side, that the F6F was working fine.[*] Even though the F8F was an improvement, the Navy didn't push production of the F8F.[†]

Captain Merrill: Exactly. From a strategic point of view, it was a good concept, because the Japs were clearly on the defensive. There was no point in complicating the war with a bunch of unproven guided missiles.

Q: What did you and Fahrney think about this change in attitude?

Captain Merrill: Fahrney felt that the assault drone program was an orphan that had been pushed too hard, especially in the beginning, when it had some 1,500 TDR-1s on order.

Q: Why did he feel that?

Captain Merrill: Mostly because both the TDR-1 and its contractor were unproved. Its prototype, the TDN, was not tested thoroughly, and the TDR had yet to fly. The "tests" in those days were more demonstrations to help sell the weapon. As an example, squadron VJ-5 had a target down on Bloodsworth Island in the Chesapeake. They hit it several times with assault drones, not with the TDR production drones, but mostly with converted conventional airplanes. Clearly, they showed that assault drones would work but did little to engender confidence in the merits of the TDR-1.

    I was not involved in the meetings between Commodore Oscar Smith and Admiral King where the decisions were made to implement the SATFOR assault drone program. By

---

[*] Grumman F6F Hellcat fighters first entered fleet squadrons in early 1943. The Hellcat was the Navy's principal carrier-based fighter plane during the last two years of World War II.
[†] Grumman F8F Bearcat fighters first entered fleet squadrons in 1945. The F8F never had much of a combat role, because it had been superseded by jets for the Korean War.

hearsay from my boss, then Captain Fahrney, I don't believe his cautionary views were sought or listened to, even if expressed.

In any case Admiral King issued directives by which 1,500 drones were ordered and the new SATFOR was created. The latter led to separate, expensive facilities at Clinton, Oklahoma, and Traverse City, Michigan. Many hundreds of officers and men reported there to train on drones that were still on Interstate's drawing boards. The SATFOR history exists in many documents, but the program can best be described as a fiasco.

However, from a 1996 hindsight viewpoint, the assault drone program can be seen as a blessing and not an embarrassment to today's Navy. I believe that the Pacific Missile Test Range, which started in October 1946, was instigated because of the strong desire of Del Fahrney and myself to ensure that future missiles would be properly tested and evaluated prior to any decision for their production and fleet deployment.

At my recommendation in 1945, the missile specialists at Traverse City were transferred to Point Mugu. Their aircraft, missiles, and support equipment went along for use in test or evaluation projects as assigned by BuAer.

Q: You mean it would have been shut down after the war was over?

Captain Merrill: Yes. But we had all these little dinky groups around the country. One of them was launching Loons at Point Mugu. It stayed out there, of course. Another was Bob Truax's liquid rocket group at Annapolis that developed the Gorgon's propulsion system.[*]

Q: Well, that was after the war, wasn't it?

Captain Merrill: Yes, this was all after the war. I'm just trying to say that another yield of the assault drone program was the head start its leftovers gave Point Mugu.

Q: Well, you talk about Jones and Smith. It's understandable that you want to see something go forward that you've worked on and are enthusiastic about.

---

[*] Lieutenant Robert C. Truax, USN.

Captain Merrill: Exactly. It is human nature to want your ideas or products to go forward. Certainly no one can doubt the dedication and patriotism of Jones and Smith. The program unraveled because of a conflict of strategic mind-sets. Unfortunately, the SATFOR group considered itself "losers," and they do to this day. They were very disappointed by the outcome and blamed a lot of the people in the fleet, i.e. the admirals who diluted their operations. The word "cabal" is used by Jones.

Q: Well, again, human nature, sometimes people think if you don't agree with me, you then are automatically wrong.

Captain Merrill: That's exactly what it is, and it's too bad. I know that Jones felt defeated, as a professional officer.

Q: And he carried that resentment for years and years afterward.

Captain Merrill: He did. I don't know if he's alive today, but his work with target drones and their conversion to assault drones deserves recognition.[*]

Q: Oscar Smith was in the class of 1908, considerably senior to both you and Fahrney.[†] Was that rank necessary and useful for pushing the program?

Captain Merrill: From Del's point of view, no. Fahrney and I were a little more tolerant of those who opposed the assault drone program. However, we tried our best to support it. Fahrney always tried to obey the orders that he got. He personally concentrated on the assault drone program and delegated me primarily to the experimental programs.

---

[*] Jones was still living at the time of this interview.
[†] Fahrney was in the Naval Academy class of 1920.

Q: Well, I'm just guessing, though, that it would have been harder for Fahrney to do his job as a commander without the support of somebody as senior as Smith.

Captain Merrill: It may well have helped. My feeling was that Smith's power was expressed through the decrees made by Admiral King. Rear Admiral Towers and many in his command structure in BuAer could not afford deliberately to dilute King's orders, but I don't think Smith's rank made a difference within BuAer.*

The Navy's seniority system often creates situations in organizations where the real brains and spark plugs are down at the middle level, and many of the others float up to the top. So the middle-level doers who have the right concepts and want to get them going have somehow to cope with that. The best way I found to cope with it was to write letters that I judged to be so damn clear and logical that they couldn't fail; some were implemented and some were not.

Very few of my letters were signed by me. But in the heading of every official naval letter one can find, in lower case, the initials of the person who wrote the letter. It helps the recipient to know that.

I once wrote a paper called "How to Write a Naval Letter." It was highly informal, but some of these points I'm trying to make are there. I started off with a section entitled "Why Bother To Learn?" Answer: "To convert your dream to an achievement." Well, it was not an official document, but it was so accepted by people that it got around by word of mouth and the power of a copier. I was out at Point Mugu in October 1996, and a guy came up to me and said "I really enjoyed that letter. I've still got a copy of it." I answered, "You're better than I am. I don't have a copy of it." So he promised to send me one.

Q: Well, I think of a comparable situation--that Draper Kauffman, out of the class of '33, was sort of the father of the underwater demolition teams, but they had a more senior captain in that group just to give them some sponsorship and visibility.†

---

* Rear Admiral John H. Towers, USN, served as Chief of the Bureau of Aeronautics from 1 June 1939 to 6 October 1942.
† The oral history of Rear Admiral Draper L. Kauffman, USN (Ret.), is in the Naval Institute collection.

Captain Merrill: Right. Well, that usually happens. Raborn was in a similar position with respect to Polaris.* He had the backing of people with such rank and power that success was almost a certainty. Who can drag his feet against the President?

Q: Did they have warheads on these drones that were tested at Bloodsworth Island?

Captain Merrill: No, they were inert. Everybody will accept the idea that if you put a live, armed warhead in there it's going to go off in a collision.

Q: On Gargoyle, what was the advantage of that type of a bomb rather than a straight iron bomb?

Captain Merrill: Two advantages: radio control gave increased accuracy and shortened the time the control plane was vulnerable to antiaircraft fire. The comparison, of course, is to conventional dive-bombing.

Q: Could you count on the same kind of accuracy with Gargoyle that you got with conventional dive-bombing?

Captain Merrill: Gargoyle was more accurate, although we never proved it until after the war. The guidance procedure was similar to but simpler than that used in the German HS-293 when it sank several ships.

Q: What other milestone steps do you remember as the war proceeded?

---

* Rear Admiral William F. Raborn, Jr., USN, was director of the Special Projects Office, which developed the Polaris submarine-launched ballistic missile system. He held the post from 1955 to 1962, being promoted to vice admiral in 1960. His Polaris oral history is in the Naval Institute collection.

Captain Merrill: My mind turns to the problems or events that arose after Fahrney left, roughly 1943. He was then a captain and, from a personnel detailing point of view, needed to go to sea. He wanted to go out and get into the war. He eventually got assigned to a logistical billet in the South Pacific, which left me in charge.

Q: Were you a commander by that point?

Captain Merrill: Yes, I was a commander. The war was drawing to a close, and some things happened that gave me new ideas. For example, after the Germans surrendered, the British took over the rocket center at Peenemunde and organized a demonstration of V-2 firings for the benefit of technical people from all the Allied countries (except the U.S.S.R.!).[*] German personnel conducted about six firings. I was detailed to go.

A party of about 10 people flew over on a DC-3, first landing in the Azores, thence to Paris and finally to Bremen.[†] I sat next to a fake Army colonel; he was a very strange sort of person. At first I didn't realize that he wasn't really a colonel; he was a great cigar smoker for one thing. All the way across the Atlantic he would smoke these stogies while ashes dropped on his uniform. Occasionally, he would halfheartedly brush them off. Now, any legitimate Army colonel will try to get all the ashes off of his coat, but not this one. He turned out to be Dr. Theodor von Karman, the famous rocket scientist from CalTech.[‡] [Laughter]

Most of us were officers of about my rank and age. But once we found out about this man, we recognized his stature and his intelligence, and we began to communicate with him, "What do you think about this thing?" and so on.

---

[*] The V-2 rocket bomb was first successfully fired on 3 October 1942 at Peenemunde, Germany. It was a liquid-fuel rocket, 46 feet long and weighing 13 tons. It carried a one-ton warhead. The German V-2 offensive against the Allies began in September 1944 and ended in March 1945; it involved some 5,000 rockets.

[†] The Douglas-built DC-3s were superb cargo or passenger planes. In World War II the DC-3 carried the Navy designation of R4D and the Army Air Forces designation C-47.

[‡] CalTech--California Institute of Technology at Pasadena. Von Karman (1881-1963) was a native of Hungary who emigrated to the United States in 1930 to pursue a career as a physicist and aeronautical engineer. He was director of thge Guggenheim Aeronautics laboratory at CalTech.

Q: So that outweighed the cigar ashes.

Captain Merrill: Yes, definitely. We tolerated the ashes better than the second-hand smoke in the confines of the airplane.

Finally, of course, we saw the Germans flawlessly fire the V-2s. We watched them closely, but the demonstration was not a learning experience for most of us. Its real importance was in bringing a group of people together with a common mind-set toward guided missiles: "We're on the leading edge of many new technologies useful to postwar guided missiles. What does it mean to the Navy? Where is my service going after the war?"

Q: The V-2 was the vertical launch.

Captain Merrill: Yes, but they were totally unguided. They just went over towards London, terrorizing the populace but killing few and creating little damage.

Q: Did they have any V-1s left that you got to see?*

Captain Merrill: No, I didn't get to see them. Peenemunde, in the German scheme of things, was tied to the Army. It handled rockets. But the German Air Force handled pilotless aircraft such as the V-1 and HS-293.

The first evening, we went to a rathskeller in Bremen for dinner. We were all sitting around, including von Karman, who had a glass of wine and was somewhat mellow. He was looking around the wall and noted a number of places where there was a light white color, compared to the wall's basic color. So he called the waiter over for an explanation.

---

* The V-1 was a pulse-jet flying bomb, also known as a "doodlebug" and "buzz bomb." It was 25 feet long and had a 16-foot wingspan. It carried a one-ton warhead some 150 miles (later increased to 250) at a speed of about 400 miles per hour. It was first successfully flown in December 1943. The Germans fired more than 13,000 V-1s during the course of World War II.

He said, "Why are these areas up here on the wall light like this? Don't you ever paint your walls?"

The waiter looked kind of sheepish, because we were Americans, and Germans were ashamed of Hitler at that point.* "Oh, the Fuhrer's pictures were there. They're not there anymore." [Laughter]

After dinner the conversation turned to future guided missiles. In retrospect I believe von Karman was the only person who was aware of the postwar prospect for nuclear warheads in ballistic missiles. Perhaps that was in his mind when turned to me and said, "Now, young man, you go home and tell them to get these rockets on ships, including the submarines.

So I said, "Yes, sir."

When I came home, I was really excited about the future. I didn't quite know how it was going to go; I certainly didn't envision what we have today. But I came back and reviewed what had already happened to an aborted 1944 proposal I had concocted with the head of ONR.† He had a research rocket program going--I can't remember the name--and he was running out of money for it. I had funds left over from the assault drone program, so I worked out a proposal where I would get some of the rockets for free. Then I would arrange to take them aboard ship and launch them, just to learn how to do it and do the research ONR wanted as well.

But I couldn't sell this one. The Chief of BuAer decided he needed the money for something else, so nothing came of that. I feel, even today, that had we gone ahead with that program, we would not have found ourselves so far behind 11 years later when it was finally recognized that the Navy should be putting ballistic missiles on submarines.

To return to my report on the V-2s, I strongly recommended that the Navy initiate a program to develop ballistic missiles for ships, including submarines. It was signed over to CNO, but nothing ever came of it.

---

* Adolf Hitler was Chancellor of Germany from 1933 until his death in 1945.
† ONR--Office of Naval Research.

Let me digress here to discuss an event, yet to happen, which uniquely affected the thinking of leaders devoted to postwar guided missiles, namely the atomic bombing of Hiroshima and Nagasaki.*

Before Hiroshima was demolished, most missileers were totally unaware that a nuclear warhead in a guided missile for use against surface targets was "just around the corner." Of paramount importance was the fact that such a warhead had roughly one million times the destructive power of an assault drone's 2000-pound bomb. Had I been able to refer to and interpret the significance of this fact to the readers of my recommendation, I doubt that they would have ignored it. My ignorance as to atomic warheads was a triumph of the wartime security system. Was it also a factor in the late start of Polaris?

Time marched on, and in the mid-'50s the idea was rediscovered by Edward Teller, I'm told, in a meeting of the President's Nobska Committee.† Its recommendation said, in essence, "The Navy is missing a great opportunity here, and you'd better set something up." That's what kicked off the Polaris program.

Q: Well, before we get into those postwar things, I've got a few other questions. One is, you were talking about the reluctance to replace proven technology with the newer things. I would think there would be a logistics problem also in getting new weapons on board carriers, where all their space is presumably dedicated to the air group. The assault drone is a case in point.

Captain Merrill: Originally, of course, when everything was hot in the assault drone program, Project Option was looking forward to getting SATFOR on aircraft carriers. But that concept was the first to go. Finally, they were just plain grounded. They had to fly out

---

* In the first combat use of atomic bombs, U.S. B-29 bombers hit Hiroshima, on the island of Honshu, on 6 August 1945 and Nagasaki, on Kyushu, on 9 August.
† Project Nobska was named for a point of land near Woods Hole, Massachusetts. Dr. Edward Teller, a highly respected Hungarian-born physicist, was the prime mover in the creation of the U.S. hydrogen bomb, which was first detonated in 1952. For details on the beginning of the program, see William F. Whitmore, "The Origin of Polaris," U.S. Naval Institute Proceedings, March 1980, pages 55-59.

of adjacent airfields against Jap targets. That was the concept that finally carried the day. So you're right, you can't put assault drones on a carrier without displacing piloted aircraft; it boils down to that.

Q: Well, there were some tests. I think the outfits were called STAG that did some work in the forward area, weren't there?[*]

Captain Merrill: Yes, there were many. At this point I need to explain that many "tests" were made by the various utility squadrons which were initially created to supply target drone services to fleet ships. With help from NAF and NRL, VJ-5 created the first assault drones by converting a number of aircraft types to radio control, some with TV and some without. Most of these were expended in mock attacks designed mostly to sell the concept rather than measure such factors as reliability, accuracy, etc. Our function in BuAer was to support them. In actual fact, we had little or no voice in these tests, although we were always invited to witness local tests. VJ-5, under Bobby Jones, developed target drones and provided support for gunnery exercises. In this capacity they served the Navy well.

As Project Option was created to accelerate the production and deployment of assault drones, it continued to make tests or mock attacks as part of the SATFOR training activities. These are well documented in two publications which I will turn over to you.[†]

Because of my limited knowledge of assault drone operations in the Pacific, I prefer to dodge your question and offer these superior sources for answers. Please note that they go beyond World War II with coverage of operations during the Korean War. Also, Bobby Jones wrote a self-published book that contains little information that is not in the foregoing sources. I sent it to Point Mugu's Missile Technology Historical Association.

Q: Did his book look forward toward future Navy requirements for assault drones?

---

[*] STAG--Special Task Air Group.
[†] "Chronology of Special Air Task Force's Story" and "Navy Drones As Combat Weapons," Captain Wynn Foster, USN (Ret.), The Hook, fall 1990 issue.

Captain Merrill: Yes, it described an operating requirement for converting mothballed, obsolete service aircraft to assault drones for suicidal attacks against heavily defended military targets. This requirement was approved just after World War II but later rescinded.

The concept focused on the fact that obsolete aircraft, which are otherwise only an expense to mothball, might be cost-effective for use against heavily defended targets. The idea was to design, produce, and store conversion kits for selected obsolete service aircraft. After conversion they would have the capabilities of today's cruise missiles, i.e., low-altitude terrain-following flight to the target with pinpoint terminal guidance. Its merit depends upon a cost comparison between Tomahawk and its competitive drone.*

Q: The engines and airframes are already paid for.

Captain Merrill: They're there, they're paid for, they're in mothballs. You would also have these conversion kits. So if, all of a sudden, you need some assault drones for a mission against Saddam Hussein, you could install these kits and be in business.† I'm not at all sure that it wouldn't be worth studying, even today

Q: Well, I remember having some correspondence with Jones in the 1980s, and one of his big goals at the time was to place a monument on some island in the Pacific where these STAG tests had been held.

Captain Merrill: Is that right?

---

* Tomahawk is a long-range cruise missile that entered the fleet in the early 1980s, capable of delivering either conventional or nuclear warheads. Originally conceived to have both antiship and land-attack versions, the antiship type is no longer in service. For details see Miles A. Libbey III, "Tomahawk," U.S. Naval Institute Proceedings, May 1984, pages 150-163.

† Saddam Hussein has been President of Iraq since 1979. In 1990 he directed Iraqi forces to invade Kuwait, leading to the U.S.-Coalition holding action, Operation Desert Shield, in 1990 and the recapture of Kuwait, Operation Desert Storm, in 1991.

Q: Well, that's my recollection. And he felt, as we mentioned, slighted and hurt because there was no recognition.

Captain Merrill: I know he felt that way. That bothers me, because I was a good friend of his, and it bothers me to admit I don't know if he's dead or not.

Q: Well, as I remember, one of his villains was Admiral Towers. What role do you remember Towers having in all of this?

Captain Merrill: My evidence is all hearsay. What I've read is that he and King hated each other, based principally on the fact that King wore an aviator's wings but never went to flight school. Frankly I don't believe this, but certainly they had very different views on Project Option--the accelerated use of assault drones. Towers, in the first phases, was Chief of BuAer and originally, according to Fahrney, accepted King's order to put this high-priority program in effect, even though Towers had recommended against it. He accepted his orders and tried his best to do the job. But he sometimes hampered the program, perhaps subconsciously. For example, there was a shortage of high-quality aluminum metal for production of aircraft. So it was decreed that the assault drones would be built out of wood, and the same for the glombs. Also, Fahrney was directed to use "new" contractors--not those that were already producing combat aircraft.

Well, the results of that were rather dramatic. For example, one of the contractors in the glomb program was Brunswick-Balke Collander, a builder of bowling alleys; they were novices at designing and producing airplanes. Of course, what they did was to go out in the job market with contract money in their pockets. They hired engineers to come in and create an engineering department. That program was not a success.

But you asked me a question about Towers. I have a tendency to wander around, as you can see.

Q: Well, sometimes the side trips are interesting too.

Captain Merrill: Back to Towers, then?

Q: And by then he was out in Hawaii.*

Captain Merrill: Yes. By then he had become totally disillusioned about assault drones. He honestly felt that SATFOR was a nuisance and that it should be taken out in any way that he could do it. He obeyed his orders, but in a halfhearted, foot-dragging way. Every time he got a chance to make a recommendation, he did, and it was negative. I do not think there was a "cabal" of officers like him that got together and knowingly tried to defeat the program.

Q: Well, and looking at it from his point of view, he had a much bigger picture, and he had a better idea of where it fit in that total picture.

Captain Merrill: Exactly. Washington should have listened to him in the beginning.

Q: How much contact did you have with the Naval Aircraft Factory during the war?

Captain Merrill: Initially, quite a bit. I found myself flying up there, learning their technology and witnessing their demonstrations. As time went on, we gave them this order for 100 TDN-1 drones. They got busy on that, flight testing the first few and delivering all pretty much on schedule. They did a good job, and all hands began to recognize that what they could do best for the Navy was to develop and test special aircraft, but not in production quantities. That policy was later embraced by changing the organization's name to Naval Air Development Center, I think they called it.

So the Special Design Branch found itself going more and more to outside contractors for the assault drones and glombs.

---

* In February 1944, as a vice admiral, Towers became Deputy Commander in Chief Pacific Fleet and Pacific Ocean Areas.

Q: Was there a test range up near Philadelphia, or where was the testing done?

Captain Merrill: Most of the testing was done by VJ-5 at NAS Cape May on the Eastern Shore. Comparing the assets available to them with those at Point Mugu today is mind boggling. Cape May is about 100 miles south of Philadelphia but it was only a short flight by air. That's where Jones's VJ-5 squadron based most of the time. A lot of target drone operations were conducted there for ships in that vicinity, and that's where much of the drone development work initially was done. Many assault drone "demonstrations" were staged out of there against targets in the Chesapeake. I found myself flying over there frequently.

Q: Did you have regular contacts with Barnaby during the course of the war?

Captain Merrill: Yes.

Q: What did those cover?

Captain Merrill: He was a sort of an informal consultant on the glomb program. He knew the technology, because he flew gliders as a personal hobby. So I would fly up to confer with him, maybe once a month. He was naturally interested in the glomb program and participated in the development of "snatch" takeoffs from a carrier deck. He had some able people, especially Lieutenant Commander Molton B. Taylor, who did most of the glomb flying. Taylor also was well versed in radio control with television guidance, a very key figure in the glomb technology.

Q: Well, I think, later in the war, Barnaby went out to the facility at Johnsville, Pennsylvania, didn't he?

Captain Merrill: Yes, I believe so. The Naval Air Development Center absorbed the various groups at NAF who were developing things rather than producing them.

Q: Did you have any connection with the program in which Joseph Kennedy, Jr., was killed, to fly against the missile sites in France?*

Captain Merrill: Yes, to a limited extent. I remember processing an order to NAF to modify a few B-24 assault drones. They had the technical skills to do it.

In the incident to which you refer, pilot Joe Kennedy was asked to attack German rocket sites which were bomb-proof and heavily defended by AA guns. I remember asking Ralph Barnaby for his opinion as to what happened. He told how Joe and his copilot took off and were flying over England, where they planned to put the drone on radio control and then bail out. At about the time they would be arming the huge torpex payload, the drone blew up violently. This, of course, put suspicion on the arming mechanism as the culprit.

Barnaby said that NAF designed the arming mechanism with a switch that activated a solenoid to insert an exploder into a torpex block. After the exploder was in place, the current to the solenoid was cut off to avoid it becoming overheated.

A subsequent and inconclusive investigation opined that STAG maintenance personnel may have wanted to be darn sure that the exploder, once in, stayed there. So they may have disengaged the cut-off feature. The result was a fast cook-off of the exploder and disaster.

By the way, this is another case where the incident was better covered in the references I listed above.

Q: Was the aircraft modified in Philadelphia before it went over to England?

Captain Merrill: Yes, I believe so.

Q: Well, really that would be an example of that conversion kit that you had talked about.

---

* Lieutenant Joseph P. Kennedy, Jr., USNR, older brother of future President John F. Kennedy. His failed mission was on 12 August 1944. For a detailed account, see Hank Searls, The Lost Prince: Young Joe, the Forgotten Kennedy; the Story of the Oldest Brother (New York: World Publishing Company, 1969).

Captain Merrill: The term "conversion kit' may be misleading. Each type of service aircraft that was converted to an assault drone had to be tailored to that type. However, the essential elements of each kit were an autopilot, a radio link (usually VHF), a decoder and actuators to behave like a pilot as to manually flying the airplane.

Today such kits would be designed to detailed Navy specs to accommodate to the operating ship and maintenance environments.

I haven't brought up the question of reliability. That was a major concern that Del Fahrney and I had about the assault and target drones, glombs, and all of the radio-controlled gadgets that we had in those days. They all depended on vacuum tubes, to start with. Solid state hadn't come into the picture and vacuum tubes were notoriously unreliable. Also, they hadn't been tested to prove their reliability, so you didn't know what you were dealing with. The operations research bean counters were totally frustrated by our inability to supply quantitative figures on how many missiles would crash from material failures before reaching their targets!

You were asking, a while back, about some of the concepts that came across to us as we went along; one of them was electronic countermeasures. There was an officer down in the BuAer electronics division who went out to Point Mugu in the late 1940s and later had a building there named for him. His name was Cliff Evans, and he was a crusader on the subject.[*] Knowing how vulnerable TV was to jamming, we supported work under him to improve things. In turn he gave us some believable figures for the RCA TVs' mean time before failure.

But it wasn't until I got out to Mugu myself that I was able to support Commander Ham Hauck and a German, Herr Doctor Robert Lusser, in making a logical study of reliability.[†] Lusser produced a book based on the probability of failure as a measure of reliability in weapon systems. It was embraced by the defense industry, and the bean

---

[*] Lieutenant Commander Clifton Evans, Jr., USN, a former enlisted man. He eventually retired in 1954 as a commander. In the autumn of 1996 the Clifton Evans, Jr., Electronic Warfare Laboratory at Point Mugu was named in his honor.
[†] Commander Hamilton O. Hauck, USN, an aeronautical engineering duty officer.

counters were happy. Today we have good reliability, because we've got solid-state components versus vacuum tubes and because we test the stuff to measure it's reliability.

Q: Do you think it's fair to describe the assault drone as a direct ancestor or predecessor of the guided missile per se?

Captain Merrill: Yes, especially if you are talking about a guided missile of the ship-launched variety. What was learned in the assault drone program filtered down through the Navy and defense industry. Those who worked with the assault drones stayed on in the Navy or moved into companies that built related missiles such as Regulus and Tomahawk.* For example, they were involved in the testing of the Tomahawk at Point Mugu, so there's a traceable transfer of experience and literature that goes back to the assault drone.

Q: Well, the intermediate stage before Tomahawk was the surface-to-air missile. Was it an ancestor of that?

Captain Merrill: No, not really. The surface-to-air missiles that later came down the track, Lark being one of them, were the earliest true surface-to-air missiles in the Navy.† They all had cruciform wings and a lot of other differences. Lark didn't look like an airplane, didn't fly like an airplane, and was designed for the job that it had to do. So I don't think there was very much carry-over of technology. There were several versions of Lark; only one of them used radio control to get up in the vicinity of the target before its radar took over.

---

* The two Regulus missiles were designed to be fired from surface ships or surfaced submarines. Regulus I, which entered the fleet in 1952, was 34 feet long, weighed 12,000 pounds, and had a speed of Mach 0.9 and range of 500 miles; Regulus II, which had its first flight test in 1958, was 57 feet long, weighed 22,000 pounds, and had a speed of Mach 2.0 and range of 1,000 miles.

† Lark was a BuAer project that originated with a 5 September 1944 memo that Commander Merrill, then head of the Special Design Branch, wrote to the Aviation Design Research Branch on the need for a surface-to-air missile to intercept enemy bombers. Although the Lark did not lead directly to an operational weapon, it provided valuable experience in the development of beam-riding guidance.

Q: Well, the initial surface-to-air missiles were beam riders, which required the ship to illuminate them on the way to the target.

Captain Merrill: Right. There were all kinds of guidance variations--semi-active, active, and so forth. These variations were barely conceived at the time of the assault drone, but we gradually appreciated them.

However, your question brings me to another point. Fahrney and I worried about promoting this translation of early technology into new guided missiles. We appreciated that the war was coming to an end and that there was going to be a "Well-now-what-do-we-do?" mind-set going around in the military and its supporting industry. Those concerned knew that there was no appreciable experience in the defense industry with guided missiles. Outfits like Lockheed didn't do much of anything with guided missiles during the war, but they knew the basic technologies that were needed. They had engineers, scientists, managers, etc. What they didn't have is the kind of money they were getting during World War II.

To cope with this problem we aimed our postwar contracts at educating such people technology-wise by putting them to work making preliminary designs of missiles we believed were both feasible and needed by the Navy. We decided to let a number of study contracts for preliminary designs of missiles specified by BuAer. Thus, their engineers would get educated on how to design guided missiles, and we'd get some solid ideas on what these guided missiles were going to look like and do and how much they would cost.

So I put together missile specifications for some 18 different study contracts that were approved by the chief. When Fahrney relieved me and I went to Point Mugu, he had a familiar blueprint to go ahead and let these contracts. Such missiles as Bullpup, Regulus, and the Sparrow family emerged from these studies. I understand that, even today, the Sparrow III is still an active missile in the Navy's arsenal.

Am I inferring that these study contracts really had a role in winning the Cold War? Definitely, and here is proof, taken from the latest issue (Summer 1997) of "Shift Colors," the BuPers newsletter for Navy retirees:

"SSBN Deterrent Patrol Insignia is now authorized for REGULUS class submarine crews who performed nuclear deterrent patrols in the late 1950s and early 1960s. . . . A belated but nevertheless, genuine congratulations is extended to all recipients." There follows a list of five submarines that made 41 patrols.* On November 2, 1962 President Kennedy announced an agreement with Soviet Premier Khrushchev that Soviet missile bases in Cuba were being dismantled.† 'Nuff said?

Q: So you were thinking already in terms of air-to-air missiles at that point.

Captain Merrill: More than air-to-air; also air-to-ground and ship-to-air. We didn't miss any of the basic types.

Q: You've talked about Jones's impatience to get the assault drones out into the fleet and Fahrney's more cautious approach. Was your thinking essentially in line with Fahrney's at that point?

Captain Merrill: Yes, I think so. I admire Jones for his energy, his salesmanship, and all of that, but what he didn't have was tolerance of the other guy's point of view. I think that's what Del Fahrney had. We wanted to get things done, but we wanted to give direction to them so they would make sense in a wartime environment; then nobody could turn them down.

Fahrney's postwar engineering contracts and the establishment of Point Mugu made so much sense at the time that there wasn't any problem of funding, let alone internal Navy opposition.

---

* The five Regulus-armed submarines were the Grayback (SSG-574), Tunny (SSG-282), Barbero (SSG-317), Growler (SSG-577), and Halibut (SSGN-687).
† In mid-October 1962, U.S. reconnaissance plane photographed a Soviet nuclear missile site in Cuba and the presence of Soviet bombers. On 22 October President John F. Kennedy went on national television to announce a naval quarantine of Cuba, to be implemented on 24 October. On 28 October Premier Nikita Khrushchev of the Soviet Union notified President Kennedy that he was ordering the withdrawal of Soviet bombers and missiles from Cuba.

Q: So you were thinking more long-range than Jones was, I would gather.

Captain Merrill: I think so.

Q: You said that Fahrney left in 1943 to go out and get into the war. Did you feel a similar desire to get out into the combat zone?

Captain Merrill: Well, yes, but I didn't let it overwhelm me. I mean by that I come from a fraternity of people that go through the Naval Academy and are taught that you're there only for one thing, and that's to be a naval officer. The first thing that a naval officer does is to qualify himself in fighting wars or preparing to fight wars. If you don't believe that, just try to get promoted. [Laughter] But my natural, personal desire was to get involved with technology. I loved technology, and that's why I put in for PG School. I knew, at that time, that I was hazarding my promotions. But that didn't mean as much to me then, nor does it now, as doing the things that I like to do and doing them well.

Q: Were you disappointed that you didn't get into a combat billet? What did you feel at the time?

Captain Merrill: Well, I wondered, when the war broke out, whether they would leave me at PG School or not. I was fully prepared for a combat assignment, since I was an experienced torpedo bomber pilot. On the other hand, I was very attracted to the embryonic guided missiles that I had heard about.

Q: Well, but I'm guessing also that so much had changed in torpedo planes between '41 and '43, you might well have been left behind had you gone out to the fleet then.

Captain Merrill: I don't think so, because when I was on the Saratoga before the war, we got the Navy's first monoplane, the TBD-1 from Douglas, as I mentioned to you before. So they were still, as far as torpedo bombers are concerned, the best in the fleet. As a matter of fact, this type of plane has since faded out of the fleet. The dive bombers have also been replaced by fighter attack planes, as I understand it.

Q: Well, I was thinking more in terms, though, of 1943. By then you would have the seniority to be a squadron commanding officer, but without the combat experience that went with that.

Captain Merrill: God only knows, but, yes, I probably would have been a squadron commander.

Q: What milestones or developments do you remember between the time Fahrney left and going over to Germany at the end of the war?

Captain Merrill: In a negative sense the dismantling of the assault drone and glomb programs was a milestone. However, the translation of its technology into later missiles and the use of some of its assets to jump-start Point Mugu was a positive milestone.

The genesis of a major milestone to come was the awarding of three contracts for development of three versions of the Lark surface-to-air guided missiles. The milestone itself occurred off Point Mugu after my tenure there. It was the world's first interception and destruction of an aircraft by a surface-launched missile.[*] The aircraft was a target drone, and the missile was Raytheon's Lark III. What follows may be inaccurate owing to fuzzy memories, but I'll go ahead anyway.

The destruction of our ships by Japanese aircraft in the early years of the war created a high-priority demand for more effective ship-based AA weapons, and both BuAer and BuOrd responded to the call. We, being of the "pilotless aircraft" mind-set, did some internal freewheeling preliminary design and issued requests for proposals to most of the qualified companies, probably in 1943.

---

[*] On 13 January 1950 a Lark fired from Point Mugu became the first guided missile to destroy an airborne target.

Three were selected, of which two survived--Fairchild and Raytheon. Progress in both camps was slower than desired. Fairchild lacked guidance experience but managed to down a drone first (by placing a radar beacon in it!). Raytheon utilized its know-how in CW radar to win the ball game. Meantime, BuOrd's team at APL brought its Bumblebee missile to fruition and eventually supplied all the surface-to-air missiles found on ships today.* BuAer's payoff came in the form of Sparrow I, a Raytheon air-to-air missile with CW radar homing.

What happened out there in the South Pacific with SATFOR assault drones had to be a milestone deserving recognition as the Navy's first combat use of guided missiles. The attacks on the Japs at Rabaul and other island installations did, at least, show that the drones could hit defended targets. No one can take that away from Bobby Jones. He was the architect of that milestone.

Other than some flight tests of Gorgon and Little Joe I don't really remember anything of "milestone" importance. Little Joe was notable in the fact that it was developed as a countermeasure to the kamikaze attacks in the Pacific. The Naval Aircraft Factory produced the first of some 15 missiles on 86 days after a go-ahead from BuAer. The missile was visually guided and radio controlled to intercept an incoming kamikaze. A flare in the tail helped in aiming, and a proximity fuze detonated a 100-pound warhead in case of a near miss. Aside from the airframe, all the components were off the shelf. Two successful launches took place on July 20, 1945. Del Fahrney described them as "the first successful flights in the United States of a surface-to-air missile in combat configuration."

Q: Well, I'm gathering that because the attack drone had sort of been turned down on large-scale combat applications that you were already looking toward postwar developments.

---

* APL--the Applied Physics Laboratory of Johns Hopkins University. "Bumblebee" was the nickname for the family of surface-to-air guided missiles being developed by the Bureau of Ordnance, as differentiated from the Lark program under the Bureau of Aeronautics.

Captain Merrill: Definitely, the emphasis was there. I've already described my paper, "Specifications for Pilotless Aircraft for Fleet Use in 1950" and its underlying purposes. But there's one other thing that happened during my last year in BuAer. That was my recommendation that the Navy establish a sea test range for guided missiles.

With all the ups and downs of previously described events, I began to get the picture that if all the planned preliminary design contracts came to fruition, or even half of them, we were going to have a tremendous amount of flight testing to do, and it should be done over the sea, for various obvious reasons. With that conviction under my belt, I drafted a letter, which the chief eventually signed out to CNO, to establish a sea test range. It suggested that a first step should be to create a board of officers to go out and find the best site and then submit a recommendation and plan for creating a range at that site.

In due time the recommendation was approved and a board of officers and civilians was formed with Captain Bowser Vieweg as its head.[*] I was detailed a member. We spent about ten days, I think, flying all over the country and down into the Caribbean looking for a sea test range. There are a number of stories involved with that odyssey, one of which, I think, is interesting.

For some reason, we didn't initially realize that Point Mugu would be even a viable candidate site. I guess it was because it's nestled down very close to a whole bunch of defense industries, and there's a lot of agriculture and small towns in the vicinity. The prospect of missile damage to that infrastructure kind of turns you off when you first think about it. But then when we really looked at it, we discovered gold. First, there's an offshore chain of islands, the Santa Barbara Channel Islands, on which you can mount your instrumentation.

There was also one isolated island some 60 miles west, called San Nicholas, which the Navy already owned. Endowed with an asphalt airstrip, it was ideal for supporting both land and sea targets as well as instrumentation. Then there was Mount Laguna about 1,100 feet high, right behind Point Mugu. From there, radar can track over the sea for hundreds of miles, and telemetry receivers can record what transpires at similar distances, line of sight, for radars and tracking stuff.

---

[*] Captain Walter V. R. Vieweg, USN.

Last, but not least, you had this infrastructure that the Seabees had put in place on the proposed air station, including Quonset huts, temporary buildings, and so forth, which were available for us to move into with our Special Weapons Tactical Test and Evaluation Unit (SWTTEU) from Traverse City Michigan.* The dismantling of SATFOR allowed the Navy to retain enough of its material and human assets to equip and staff SWTTEU. Let me describe this unique organization as it then existed.

While in BuAer, I was instrumental in getting a classmate, then-Commander Ernest Christensen, to go out there and take command of SWTTEU. He organized personnel from SATFOR, NAF, and the fleet assigned by BuPers to flesh out some 220 people with varying experience or backgrounds for missile testing.† They inherited drones, glombs, and Gorgons that were scheduled for tests and kept them busy pending the outcome for Point Mugu.

Meanwhile, the board's recommendation, which I wrote, nominated Point Mugu and submitted a plan for its implementation. It was supported widely in the Navy Department but had to be coordinated with the other services. Finally it was approved by President Truman and big bureaucratic wheels began to turn.‡ SWTTEU was moved temporarily into the vacated NAS Mojave. Bob Truax's rocket test group and the Loon flight test unit were moved directly to Point Mugu.§ On October 1, 1946 the Naval Air Missile Test Center was officially commissioned at Point Mugu.

Q: Well, I believe your letter is regarded as a really instrumental milestone in that process.

Captain Merrill: I guess so. I spent an awful lot of time on it.

---

* Seabees is the name universally applied to members of the Navy's mobile construction battalions (CBs). A Quonset hut is a semi-cylindrical metal building that can be shipped to an advance base area and erected quickly.
† BuPers--Bureau of Naval Personnel.
‡ Harry S Truman served as President of the United States from 12 April 1945 to 20 January 1953.
§ Loon was the U.S. Navy's version of the German V-1 self-propelled bomb. It was first intended as a ship-to-shore bombardment weapon. Later it was used as a platform for general missile development in the areas of propulsion, guidance, control, and launching techniques.

Q: I can imagine you did.

Captain Merrill: And Melanie Holmes, this young lady Naval Reserve yeoman that I mentioned, is the one that typed it all up and later became a captain.

Q: One question we haven't talked at all about during this wartime period is security of classified information. How tightly held was the work on your programs?

Captain Merrill: It was very tight, especially in the beginning. You would have thought that we were developing the atomic bomb. Everything was classified secret or confidential; the category "top secret" had yet to be invented. In retrospect, it was almost ridiculous, because the things that were being worked on were nothing more than pieces of hardware that were pulled out of the various aircraft programs and modified. The one possible exception would be the U.S. Navy's interest in airborne television as produced by RCA. Television technology was public knowledge; nothing classified about that.

To digress briefly, we were very concerned about the vulnerability of television to jamming; it's a wide-open communication system. If assault drone operations had occurred earlier in the Pacific, as Oscar Smith hoped, it wouldn't have taken the Japs long to figure out how to jam the television link. We were very concerned about that. As far as counter-countermeasures go, they're still very difficult.

Q: Wasn't television also part of that mission that Joseph Kennedy was on?

Captain Merrill: Oh, yes. His job was to guide a drone onto V-2 rocket sites, and he had to have precision guidance to do it. TV was vital to his mission.

Q: Was static electricity ever considered as one of the causes of his plane's premature explosion?

Captain Merrill: I don't remember hearing about it. I don't think so. It seemed almost certain that deliberate closing of the arming switch initiated the explosion. I'm pretty sure that static electricity was not involved.

Q: Well, I would think that even though you didn't get to the combat zone during World War II, you have one very obvious benefit, and that's being able to spend the whole war with your family.

Captain Merrill: Yes, I was thankful for that. In 1942 we bought a three-bedroom house down in Falls Church, Virginia, for $11,000. And we were able to hire a young woman to come in and help with the housekeeping.

Q: How much time were you able to spend with the family with this work schedule you had?

Captain Merrill: The main absences, of course, were associated with traveling. I would say that I was on the road one day for every ten that I would be in the office. It wasn't a burden really, and much of the traveling was combined with proficiency flight training where I flew the plane myself.

    I seldom returned home from the office before 6:00 P.M., thus burdening my sainted wife.

Q: What sort of plane did you use for those trips?

Captain Merrill: It was called a JRC. It was a Cessna two-seater light plane with a capacity for about three passengers.

Q: Did you have to put up with the same rationing limitations that civilians did during that period?

Captain Merrill: Oh, no. This, of course, was considered military flying because I was keeping my proficiency up and attending to Navy business. On other hand, we were loosely limited to about six hours per month. So we weren't wasting gas.

Q: Well, I was thinking, though, more in terms of food rationing and gasoline rationing for your car.

Captain Merrill: Well, of course, we shared with the general public on all those things; I don't remember it as a hardship. Everybody was doing it, and we just accommodated to the rules.

Q: What sort of recreational activities did you do with the family during that time?

Captain Merrill: Well, we got pretty enamored of boating at about that time. I bought a small sailboat from an Air Force colonel. He had gotten a set of plans from Popular Mechanics and built this boat out of unseasoned 2x4 lumber and plywood. So you can imagine what kind of a sailboat it was. But it floated, and it got us where we wanted to go. We did a lot of cruising on the Eastern Shore from a marina in Annapolis. We sweated out one hurricane anchored in St. Mary's Creek over on the Eastern Shore. I wrote several magazine articles on this and other adventures.

Q: What do you remember about the atmosphere in wartime Washington?

Captain Merrill: I recall the hard work and high dedication of the people that I worked with. There was a "can do" spirit and a underlying patriotism that I haven't seen since. It was infectious. It was a general commitment to winning the war that nobody argued with. Of course, there were those who took advantage and profited unduly from the war. But, in general, I was quite impressed by how people were committed to winning the war.

Q: Did you wear your uniform to work every day?

Captain Merrill: Yes, I remember doing that. It changed later, of course, after the war was over.

Q: Well, and I think before the war also, civilian clothes were the norm for Navy people stationed in Washington.

Captain Merrill: I guess they were. I seldom visited Washington before the war.

Q: Any other people from BuAer or your section specifically that you'd like to mention from the wartime period?

Captain Merrill: One of the things that I came away with was an appreciation for the Naval Reserve volunteers who came in and served there, either as officers or, in some cases, as civilian engineers. They worked right along with and just as hard as the regular Navy people. In fact, the regular Navy was definitely in the minority. On the other hand, the leadership of most operations there was still in the hands of the regular Navy. It seemed natural to both categories since the reservists were less concerned with promotion.

Q: Well, that split was parallel to what was in the fleet at that time. Most of the people were reservists, but the leadership were regular Navy.

Captain Merrill: That's right. It's a good combination. The reservists brought lots of good things with them, especially industrial or academic experience; also a little more tolerance and humor. The regular Navy, on the other hand, was inclined toward formality, discipline, and so on. But the dedication was equal.

Q: Anything else about the wartime period to mention?

Captain Merrill: I've already described Little Joe, our effort to deal with the kamikaze threat. I should add that the atomic attack on Hiroshima and Nagasaki accelerated closure on the war and overtook the requirement for Little Joe. It finally was flight tested a few times and then canceled in favor of the Lark and Bumblebee developments.

Q: In July '45, Vice Admiral Willis Lee was called back from the Pacific, and he set up an experimental task force in Casco Bay, Maine, specifically to deal with the kamikaze threat, because there was concern about the upcoming invasion of Japan that was planned for that fall.[*] Did you have any dialogue or contact with his organization?

Captain Merrill: No, I didn't. In fact, it's news to me about this. Of course, my role was not very intimate in it. I sent the Little Joe project up to Philadelphia, and they did the work. I monitored the work, so to speak.

Q: Well, just a couple of things I recall that his group worked with. One would be a moving target indicator radar, so that the contacts would stand out if they were coming out from over land. And another was flak bursts that had some sort of colored powder in them so that you could tie a specific gun to a specific flak burst, sort of the way they did with dyes in gun projectiles.

Captain Merrill: Not a bad idea at all.

Q: On the proximity fuze, of course, the Johns Hopkins Applied Physics Lab had a lot of role in that. Did you have any tie with their organization?

Captain Merrill: We had personal contacts and followed their work, in spite of security barriers. I worked with Merle Tuve on the proximity fuze, for example.[†] He was a top

---

[*] Vice Admiral Willis A. Lee, Jr., USN.
[†] Dr. Merle A. Tuve was instrumental in the development of the proximity fuze for 5-inch antiaircraft projectiles. It was also known as the VT, or variable time fuze. For a detailed

manager over there, a major influence, Whenever we had any problems, I contacted him. APL did a lot of things for BuOrd. They were doing a lot of interesting things over there.

Q: How much liaison did your organization have with the Bureau of Ordnance?

Captain Merrill: Pretty close. I mentioned the closeness of Dundas Tucker to Fahrney. I tried to continue this liaison and did various things for them. For example, they had an air-to-surface infrared homing guided missile. It homed on heat radiation, presumably coming from a ship. They wanted to test it against a maneuvering target simulating a ship. So I set up a project at NAF. They acquired a huge truck and lined the open cargo space with firebrick. This space was then converted to a fire-box as found under the boiler of an oil-fired ship. When sited on a dry lake near Inyokern, the truck would look like a ship to an infrared sensor.* The final piece-de-resistance was to make the truck radio controlled, thus simulating a maneuvering ship on a dry lake!

The truck eventually arrived at Inyokern, but what happened to it after that, I don't know. You could say, "Why did you waste all that money on it?" The answer, "It was BuOrd money."

Here's an interesting postscript on this project. One day a British naval officer, searching for a similar target for his similar missile, came into the office and asked for a briefing on our maneuvering truck. He was a typical dour skeptic. After my presentation he said, "The technical brilliance of this truck blinds one to its utter uselessness."

We did things for BuOrd, they did things for us, like the proximity fuze.

Q: Well, I would say that you didn't know in advance which things were going to work and which weren't, so you had to test them to protect your investment.

Captain Merrill: Exactly.

---

account, see Buford Bowland and William R. Boyd, U.S. Navy Bureau of Ordnance in World War II (Washington, D.C.: U.S. Government Printing Office, 1953), pages 271-290.
* Naval Ordnance Test Station, Inyokern, California.

Q: I wonder if that had any connection with the later heat-seeking guidance systems.

Captain Merrill: Oh, yes. This missile was, to my knowledge, the first heat-seeking air-to-surface guided missile in the Navy.

Q: Were there other examples of such cooperation?

Captain Merrill: Yes. About the time SWTTEU was set up in Traverse City we were was able to latch onto some 15 German Askania photo theodolites, precision instrumentation cameras. They were shipped from Germany to SWTTEU at Traverse City and thence to NAS Mojave. There we realized that the theodolites were not in good condition and had to be overhauled. SWTTEU had no facilities for this, but the people at NOTS, Inyokern, being fellow guided missile pioneers, overhauled them for us. I guess they charged us money for it, but we got them back in good shape--just in time for testing some of our glombs out in the Mojave Desert.

Q: On your trip to Germany you mentioned the incident of going into the rathskeller with the pictures gone. What other recollections do you have of Germany, such as lodging arrangements and contact with the German people?

Captain Merrill: We really didn't have much contact with them. I think we stayed one night in a German hotel, probably that same night. We went in, saw the demonstrations, and then flew home. The Japanese kamikaze problem awaited most of us.

Q: How long was the whole trip, would you say?

Captain Merrill: We landed our DC-3 in the Azores on the way over and went on to land in Paris. It wasn't too much of an exercise--two days over, two days back, one or two days to see the demonstrations. No more than six days, I would say.

Q: Of course, a number of the German scientists came to work in the United States such as von Braun.*

Captain Merrill: Right.

Q: How did those ties develop that brought those people to this country?

Captain Merrill: I'm glad you brought you up. That's a story that certainly belongs in this oral history and elsewhere.

There was a program, probably initiated by the Army, called Paper Clip. The name doubtless reflected the fact that it involved much red tape. [Laughter] The idea was for each armed service to send a recruiting team to go in behind our troops as they captured regions in which guided missile scientists were located. You might say they had a buyers' market.

The group I later became close to at Point Mugu told me they were overjoyed at the opportunity to work for the U.S.A., especially since they eventually would be joined by their families.

As you've mentioned, Wernher von Braun and his group kept their identity in the Army. They were brought over by the Army, and put to work almost immediately as a group. The Navy team focused on a scientist by the name of Dr. Herbert Wagner, whom I've already mentioned. He enjoyed a stature with the German Air Force similar to von Braun's with the Army. So the Navy put its finger on Dr. Wagner and about 15 of his assistants or industrial affiliates. All were well-chosen scientists or engineers.

The Navy's initial assimilation of its contingent was uninspired, to my way of thinking. In the beginning, it placed these people in a special devices development facility on Long Island under the Office of Naval Research. The concept was that they were there

---

* Wernher von Braun was a German-born rocket scientist who helped develop rockets for his country in World War II, then emigrated to the United States in 1945 and began working with the Army. He subsequently played a considerable role in the U.S. space program.

to be brainwashed by our scientists and engineers from both the defense industry and the Navy. Thus they would learn all about German guided missiles.

Well, the Navy gave a party and nobody came. You know how human professionals are. They usually think, "Well, I know it anyway. Besides, it's a nuisance to go up there only to find that they don't speak English." That situation lasted for some two to three months while they were totally unhappy.

I followed this situation until one day I talked to the Chief of Naval Research, who jelled my interest in seeing if we could get them to come out to Point Mugu. So I went up there and interviewed them--Wagner and several of the others. That confirmed my feeling that they and we would prosper if we could just get them out to Point Mugu. So I wrote a letter asking for that. As usual, it was for someone else to sign.

Q: That's the Navy way.

Captain Merrill: Yes, probably a good thing in the end.

Q: Who signed the letter?

Captain Merrill: I think it was Captain Hatcher, then Commander, NAMTC.[*] This was after the war, of course. It was approved, and in due time they were on their way, many with their families.

After conferring with my technical people, we decided not to use them as a group. We would instead spread them around where their skills could best be used. That meant that they would work in separate groups within the organization, separate offices, etc. It proved to be a good decision as they were rapidly assimilated, forced to use English, and gradually made friends with former enemies. In a few months they became key players.

One problem remained. They still had a lot of immigration hurdles with much paperwork, housing, schools, and so on. So I picked out an officer, a sociable lieutenant

---

[*] Captain Robert S. Hatcher, USN, served as Commander Naval Air Missile Test Center from April 1947 to June 1949.

whose name was Sidney Sharp, and gave him the responsibility of a guidance counselor for the whole group, including their families.* A deep-seated affection developed between him and his charges, which still exists.

Q: Did Lieutenant Sharp speak German?

Captain Merrill: No, which was probably best, Most of them spoke some English, Wagner especially. Others quickly learned; they knew that they had to learn English, so they went to adult schools and sent their kids to public schools. They were top-notch people. None returned to Germany, to my knowledge.

Q: Was there any concern about reliability, since these people had been working for the Nazi regime?

Captain Merrill: Yes, initially, and that's why they isolated them at first. They couldn't imagine that these people could change their allegiances overnight. But that's exactly what they did. None of them had any respect for the Nazi regime, that I ever discovered. I don't know of any time that they offered anything but criticism for Nazism.

Q: Well, that's about what you would expect, of course.

Captain Merrill: Oh, yes. Of course, they had no other option, you might say.

Q: Well, I mean, even if they had been in support of the Nazis, they were probably not going to say it at that point.

Captain Merrill: Amen to that.

---

* Lieutenant Sidney A. Sharp, USN.

Q: Did you have any concerns for your physical safety when you were in Germany for that period?

Captain Merrill: No. We were in a group. Ostensibly we were all military, except for von Karman. Anybody could see he was non-military. I think the hotel we went to had been commandeered by the military. I had the feeling, from the few contacts that I had there, as in this rathskeller, that there was great relief on the Germans' part to have the whole era over with. "Take Hitler's pictures down and get on with your life." So I wasn't fearful at all.

Q: There was another mission called the Alsos Mission that went over there looking for submarine technology, for example.* Did you have any links with that group?

Captain Merrill: No, I didn't, probably because it was just a different technology. In fact, I just learned it from you. [Laughter]

Q: Were you aware of any comparable effort towards the Japanese once they had been defeated?

Captain Merrill: No, I never heard of any such program. I don't know why. Maybe there was no such effort ever made.

Q: Was part of your job to gather up stocks of their missiles such as the V-1 and V-2 and ship them to the United States?

Captain Merrill: No. I wasn't involved in that. I knew that others were interested in getting the V-1 going in the Army Air Corps. Actually they were well on their way before the war ended and before the Navy got seriously interested. Finally, Fahrney contacted his

---

* See the Naval Institute oral history of Rear Admiral Albert G. Mumma, USN (Ret.). An excerpt on the Alsos Mission appeared in Naval History, Summer 1989, pages 51-53.

Army Air Corps friend, Colonel Holloman, and set the stage for the Navy to buy some 100 V-1 buzz bombs. We called them Loons. The concept, of course, was to launch them from ships against Japanese targets.

Of course, the war with Japan was still on; we had that war still to win. That fact justified the Air Corps in going ahead with its program to copy the V-1 and produce it in large numbers for air or ground launching. I believe Chrysler was the contractor. Initially we were supposed to get 100, but I think we wound up getting more than that. Loons were never fired in anger, but they proved to be great test platforms, a learn-while-you-do missile. Loon firings at Point Mugu provided a number of sea stories.

Q: How were the Loons modified?

Captain Merrill: In the beginning the only modification was to make them radio controlled for safety during flight tests.

There were two ways of launching them. One involved a catapult that was especially built by some Navy facility. It was a "powder" catapult that had a long tube, slotted at the top to facilitate a link between a powder-driven piston and a cart bearing the Loon. Along this tube were some JATO bottles fitted in so that they would fire off sequentially as the piston went down the tube. The resulting acceleration environment was tough on the Loons, especially when we added more delicate guidance components later on.

The alternate launcher used two short rails bearing a cart with the Loon above. JATO bottles powered this assembly off the rails and well into flight. Then it fell off and the Loon continued under its own pulse jet power. This alternate was obviously the only choice for surfaced submarines and soon eclipsed the catapult.

Shortly after the war and after he became CNO, Admiral Nimitz, surely the Navy's number one submariner, paid Point Mugu a visit.[*] He wanted to see a Loon fired from a submarine. We were able to schedule it from the Cusk.[†]

---

[*] Fleet Admiral Chester Nimitz, USN, served as Chief of Naval Operations from 15 December 1945 to 15 December 1947.
[†] The first launch of a missile from a submarine was a Loon fired from the USS Cusk (SS-348) off Point Mugu on 12 February 1947.

The admiral flew in on time, was properly greeted, and then embarked on an AVR boat so that he could be close to the submarine but still far enough away not to be endangered by a possible explosion from the JATOs.* Back in the control center we crossed our fingers because we had had one or two failures out of, say, five or six prior launches. As usual, we had a fighter that came in behind the Loon to shoot it down in case we didn't have control of it.

All of the preflight operations went like clockwork. The pulse jet started, and they pulled the trigger on the sub. The Loon took off in great shape, dropped its launching cart, and then greeted us with dead silence as it glided away; the pulse jet had stopped! I expected it to stall and dive into the sea, but on it went in silent dignity. While I imagined the look of disgust on the admiral's face, the Loon disappeared into a fog bank lurking just off the beach

What Admiral Nimitz thought of this whole fracas I never found out. But anyone smart enough to defeat the Japanese fleet would surely know what failed and that it was unimportant in the whole scheme of things.

Q: Well, I take it it was supposed to fly for a longer period than that before it fell into the sea.

Captain Merrill: Oh, yes. If the engine had continued, we had planned to fly it out some 50 miles to Begg Rock, using beach radar and radio control, and dump it on the target. We had previously done this successfully, hitting within 60 feet of the rock.

Q: That's impressive.

Captain Merrill: It was, especially in those early days. So this was a failure? Yes, everything was spectacular about it except it didn't succeed.

Q: How far did it go in comparison with the 50 miles that were expected?

---

* AVR--aircraft rescue vessel.

Captain Merrill: I don't remember, possibly two or three miles at the most. The autopilot was keeping it nice and level, but sooner or later it had to stall.

Q: Could you describe, please, the wrapping up of your activities in Washington? What else happened before you got relieved?

Captain Merrill: I think Del and I had two or three weeks to discuss ongoing projects such as the various active missiles, the logistics of staffing and locating what was to be the NAMTC, Point Mugu, and the approved list of new missiles to be started as engineering studies. In my speech in April, 1984 at Point Mugu I listed the convictions we both had as to what BuAer should do after the war:

1. Neither the Axis nor Allied guided missiles made a decisive impact on the war's outcome.
2. There was a strong consensus, however, that guided missiles could greatly augment the fleet's fighting capabilities.
3. The defense industry serving the Navy and our own personnel needed more education on missile technology, especially the more advanced German concepts.
4. The advent of nuclear warheads gave missiles a destructive power which more than offset their complexity and expense; a marriage was inevitable.
5. Prospective postwar budgets and a worldwide yearning for peace suggested that we had time to pause and work out missile specifications prior to their development.

After I left, there was not much verbal communications between us, because he was busy managing the above projects, and I was busy testing the World War II guided missiles as well as creating, staffing, and managing the technical organization at Mojave and Point Mugu. Del had to deal with the reservists leaving the Navy. At first he had to operate with a smaller staff but soon found good replacements and kept right on going. Commander John Leydon was his deputy and later became the leading expert and advocate for Point Mugu when it was endangered by the ambitions of competing services.*

---

* Commander John K. Leydon, USN.

A final discussion of our operations with target drones is appropriate before we leave Washington. I've already discussed how they were predecessors to the assault drones and dramatically focused attention on fleet AA defense shortcomings. The advent of small target drones needs attention.

One day, about 1943, a small, dapper man named Reginald Denny came into my office. He was, of course, a well-known movie actor at that time. He also was a hobbyist who pioneered small radio-controlled airplanes with wing spans of about six feet. He and some capitalists had formed a company called "Radioplane" in Van Nuys, California, and had convinced the Air Corps to buy some for use as targets for .50-caliber machine guns and small caliber AA guns, say 3-inch. I quickly became convinced that we should obtain some for test and evaluation. This we did, again with the help of Colonel Holloman.

While awaiting delivery, we needed to set up a small group within SWTTEU to test and evaluate them. Now, it so happened that my sister was married to an ensign reservist named Kip Tuttle, who was awaiting assignment to duty.[*] I knew his qualifications and was able to have him sent to SWTTEU for this job.

Under Kip's dynamic leadership, the TDD (target drone, Denny) became the first in a still-existing line of small target drones. At first, Kip's team went aboard each ship to be served, complete with a rubber-powered catapult and several TDDs. The ship then put to sea, and Kip confronted the AA gunners with a target that flew very much like an attacking aircraft. Later the catapult was installed on an AVR boat which accompanied the ship to sea. Success came quickly.

At Point Mugu the target drone department expanded along with the contractors who developed faster, more sophisticated target drones--mostly launched from utility aircraft

Q: Of course, another problem, after the war ended was that the money faucets stopped flowing freely.

Captain Merrill: Very definitely.

---

[*] Ensign Melbourne W. Tuttle, USNR.

Q: So in addition to losing people, he was losing money.

Captain Merrill: Yes, but his need for money was alleviated by the nature of his work. It lacked the costly production aspect; he was doing R&D work.[*] This changed as time went on. The Special Design Branch became a true weapons supplier after Del passed the baton to other leaders. The Lark, Regulus, Rigel, Bullpup, the air-to-air Sparrow missiles and others came down the line.

Q: At what point did you move from Washington to Point Mugu?

Captain Merrill: Shortly after the war ended, about September 1945. I went first to NAS Mojave, because that's where the center of gravity was, and shortly after that I went on down to Point Mugu.

Q: Well, you described writing the letter that made the case for using Point Mugu for this purpose. Who then had to bless and approve that?

Captain Merrill: That letter went up the chain of command in the Navy Department and finally was approved, in its premises, by President Truman. In that process it was coordinated with naval commands who had an interest and the other armed services. President Truman approved it, because it involved the taking of civilian lands. That approval removed all foot-dragging within the executive branch of government and permitted the Navy to implement the decision without further hindrance.

Q: We can get the rest of that story in our next interview.

Captain Merrill: Great.

---

[*] R&D--research and development.

Interview Number 3 with Captain Grayson Merrill, U.S. Navy (Retired)

Place: Captain Merrill's home, Annapolis, Maryland

Date: Friday, 17 January 1997

Interviewer: Paul Stillwell

Q: Captain, it's a pleasure to see you this morning in the warmth of your office on this cold, cold day outside. I hope you had a pleasant holiday since our last meeting.

Captain Merrill: Yes to all of those things, and ready to go.

Q: When we left off last time, which was in November, you were just winding up your tour in BuAer in Washington, moving out and getting Point Mugu established. What steps did you take once you got out there?

Captain Merrill: Well, getting out there involved flipping my car over after a New Mexico ice storm, so the first thing I had to do was to get it repaired. After that, of course, I reported in at NAS Mojave where most of the work and planning was located.

Q: Probably late 1945 or early '46.

Captain Merrill: Yes, it would probably be in the winter of '45.
    The only group that was operating at Point Mugu was the Loon detachment. They had to be down there from the very beginning of their operation because they had a heavy catapult launcher that had to be on the beach. They were operating under the auspices of the Seabees, who were in the process of shutting their activities down and getting ready for us to move in. So the center of gravity, so to speak, was up at the Naval Air Station Mojave. It was called the Special Weapons Tactical Test and Evaluation Unit (SWTTEU), under the command of Commander Ernest E. Christensen. The total population was about 200.

Most of the testing had to do with the early weapons such as the glombs, assault drones, Gorgons and Azons. We also had a few of the TDRs from the defunct SATFOR program.

Q: How far was the air station at Mojave from Point Mugu?

Captain Merrill: By line of sight, I would guess 60 miles, but driving between them involved winding, up and down roads over the mountains. So it was probably a 90-minute drive.

Q: How much of an establishment was there at Point Mugu per se?

Captain Merrill: There were quite a few temporary buildings, such as Quonset huts and prefab offices built for training Seabees during the war. There was also a short Marston mat runway with a couple of prefab hangars alongside.* At the beach were a sturdy fishing pier, a respectable prefab officers' club, and about six beach cottages.

All these were very enticing to the Mojave people who were eager to move down to a more equitable climate for both work and recreation. It was very fortunate that the Seabees were retrenching at Point Mugu but staying on at Port Hueneme, because they had all the skills necessary to maintain, modify, and even expand the temporary facilities we needed before the permanent facilities could be brought on line. They also saw us as relatively well-heeled Navy customers!

Q: About how long a hiatus was there between their departure and your getting going?

Captain Merrill: Well, it was a continuous process, but it started just about the time I got there. They were winding down their activities and taking people out, moving them back

---

* Marston mat consisted of prefabricated alumimum strips that were longitudinally ribbed for strength and perforated with rows of holes for lightness. They were used by the Army and Navy to construct advance airstrips during World War II. The matting was first used in 1941 Army maneuvers near the town of Marston, North Carolina.

over to Port Hueneme. The Loon detachment of which I spoke, had, I would guess, around 60 people associated with it. So it was a very modest operation. But even before I got there, certain activities were scheduled to move in. For example, the rocket unit under Commander Robert Truax moved directly from Annapolis down to the beach, because, of course, they needed safe isolation for their rockets. Shortly after my arrival we started a phased move of the NAS and SWTTEU activities down to Point Mugu. This was about 85% completed by the date of commissioning for NAMTC on October 1, 1946.

The move was fairly fluid, because everything we owned we could put in Seabee trucks. Of course, there was a buildup of personnel that happened at the same time, and accommodating those incoming people involved a lot of housekeeping, such as putting them temporarily in buildings at Mojave and then moving them and their families down to Point Mugu or wherever they could find housing.

Q: Were government quarters available for these people?

Captain Merrill: Yes, there were a few government quarters that were usable, mostly Quonset huts. But, in general, the people rented homes and moved into Oxnard and Camarillo.

Q: So was the air station at Mojave then progressively shut down?

Captain Merrill: Yes, It was progressively shut down. About the time I got there, it was no longer in the hands of the Marine Corps. They had completely turned it over to SWTTEU and the Naval Air Station Mojave was set up. Captain Scoles took that over, and I administered the various technical operations.* There was considerable organizational restructuring going on that we had to deal with. Common sense took over. The people

---

* Captain Albert Scoles, USN, was commanding officer of the Pilotless Aircraft Unit from November 1945 to September 1946; the PAU did the early Loon testing. When the Naval Air Missile Test Center was commissioned in October 1946, the first commander was Captain Albert N. Perkins, USN. He was relieved in January 1947 by Captain Scoles, who was in command until April 1947.

that could do certain things were asked to do them, and the other people stayed out of their hair. I'm speaking especially about Bud Scoles, with whom I was quite friendly.

Q: Were you the officer in charge of the missile unit then?

Captain Merrill: Yes, the former SWTTEU, the Loon detachment, and the rocket group as it filtered in.

Q: So how much autonomy did you have in that role?

Captain Merrill: Well, I never felt constrained in any way. I felt that I was given all the help that I could possibly expect from the air station. I was friends with Bud Scoles, and my classmate, Ernie Christensen, had been sent to sea duty.[*]

An interesting thing happened at about that time. The Washington detailers, who worry about protocol, realized that no other naval air station was under the command of an AEDO, an aeronautical engineering duty only officer, namely Bud Scoles. So Bud was relieved by Captain Perkins, a line officer, a fine gentleman who was on his last tour before retirement. He was totally unfamiliar with guided missiles. Nevertheless, he ran a good air station, from an administrative point of view.

Q: Well, if he just let you alone to do your work, that would be a good thing.

Captain Merrill: Yes, although he often went the extra mile for us, as an example scrounging up trucks that were then being sold off by the Navy or put in storage.

Q: Did that downsizing cause you any problems in terms of getting personnel or funding?

---

[*] Christensen commanded the Special Weapons Tactical Test and Evaluation Unit from August 1943 to November 1945, when Scoles took command of the Pilotless Aircraft Unit.

Captain Merrill: No, it didn't really. The detailers were looking around for assignments for good people. Also, they were responsive to nominations we made from our personal experiences. We got some very fine talent assigned to us at this time.

Q: Any examples you remember?

Captain Merrill: There was Lieutenant Sidney Sharp of whom I previously spoke, Also, I was helped in recruiting Ralph Peterson from BuAer, a civilian who later became the first Director of Laboratories.

The important aspect, which you alluded to, is that being in a downsizing environment was a big advantage to us. A stellar example of that was our acquisition of SCR-584 tracking radars. When we heard some were available at an Army depot in Sacramento, we quickly organized a unit of men and trucks to go there and "liberate" at least three. These were very important to us in those days, because they were the only means we had for tracking aircraft and missiles out over the sea range.

Q: Were they regular air-search radars?

Captain Merrill: No, actually they were fire-control radars, used effectively for AA defense during the Battle for Britain. They were also effective in directing fighters against buzz bombs. I understand the Army Signal Corps made copies for the Air Corps. In the end, we got about six of those radars. They were a very important part of our instrumentation.

Q: Well, you knew which direction you were shooting the missiles, so you knew which direction to train the fire-control radar.

Captain Merrill: Yes. We usually knew approximately where the aircraft or missile of interest was and the radar's beam was wide enough to acquire a target in a specified sector.

This seems a good time to tell the story of how the SCR-584 AA fire control radar became the Navy's first close-air fighter support control system.

As you know, the Loon missile, a copy of the German buzz bomb, was seen initially by the Navy as a submarine-launched missile aimed at Japanese beachhead fortifications. Its radar beacon was tracked by the sub's radar, and it was guided to and dumped on the target by radio control. For safety during tests off Point Mugu we had an armed F6F fighter escorting the missile. If any threat to persons or valuable property occurred, test control told the fighter to shoot it down.

The Marines were interested in the project because they would quite likely be future targets. Consequently they furnished a detachment of several fighters under the command of a colorful captain nicknamed "Dirty" Dalby.[*]

One day Dirty drifted into my office to complain mildly about the lack of any projects devoted to the Marine Corps. He was itching to get more involved, as was his cadre of skilled technicians. I knew he was flying Loon simulation missions for Dr. Wagner, who was then modifying the SCR-584 radar and developing a command computer to yield a warhead arming signal and a dump command. As we chatted, we both realized that what we were sitting on was an embryonic all-weather close-air support system the Marines had long dreamed about but not asked for. He was a can-do type personified, so I designated him as project manager of an in-house bootleg project to develop a prototype system.

In a few weeks Dirty's fighters were dropping inert bombs on a buoy offshore with a CEP accuracy of 30 yards.[†] The time had come to dignify the project with Washington approval. Soon thereafter, Del Fahrney in BuAer approved the project and notified CNO of its future potential.

The Marines got justifiably excited about this and sponsored a back-up BuAer contract with General Electric for a mil-spec version called (I believe) APQ-2. Shortly, the Korean War came along and Dirty Dalby's team, with its prototype system, went overseas and acquitted themselves nobly. Today, newer generations of close-air-support systems for attack fighters are a critical element in ground combat.

---

[*] Captain Marion C. Dalby, USMC.
[†] CEP--circular error probable.

Q: Well, how did it work precisely? Was there some kind of a beacon that was connected with the target, or how was it acquired?

Captain Merrill: You see, it's a front-line support concept, so you've got Marines up there, and across the lines you've got the Koreans. If the weather is foul but flyable, the system is especially effective. Obviously, our troops have close contact with the enemy, so they know where the target is. Under the close-air support concept, they're in charge of designating the target and its coordinates to the ground radar crew.

Q: Like a forward air controller.

Captain Merrill: Exactly. He then calls for fighter support. Once the fighters are airborne and acquired by the forward controller, they can fly over or in the overcast and still deliver bombs on the targets

Q: Sort of like a beacon, then.

Captain Merrill: It's analogous to that. The forward controller knows the target coordinates and sends them to the control group. An actual beacon is not used.

Q: Why do you call it a bootleg project?

Captain Merrill: The Navy is well aware of the defense industry's opposition to in-house developments which compete with the defense companies' capabilities. This is a complicated policy issue, but BuAer, in those days, elected not to do development in those of its facilities assigned to testing defense industry products, be they systems or a black box. So this Marine project was a recognized departure from policy. It happened by tacit agreement between Del Fahrney, then in BuAer, and me--two "bootleggers," if you will. As soon as its merit became evident, we mainstreamed the project, and no one ever objected.

Q: What other contributions did you get from the German scientists?

Captain Merrill: Well, there was a German by the name of Willie Ley who was in charge of the launching systems for the Loon. The actual hardware was designed by contractors under the Bureau of Aeronautics, but a lot of improvements were needed, and he was able to lead that. I was told that he actually piloted a V-1 buzz bomb for the German Air Force so his job was somewhat ironic.

Incidentally, after I became the first technical director of the Polaris project, I was instrumental in bringing him into the program. At Lockheed he was in charge of the submerged launching of that missile from submarines.

Q: It sounds as if the Germans were completely cooperative in this venture.

Captain Merrill: Oh, they were. They were just people, like everybody else. I think that the Germans were sold a bill of goods by Hitler and company. Once they got trapped into the Nazi dictatorship they couldn't get out, so they did what they felt they had to do. As soon as Germany was defeated, they were only too happy to immigrate to the United States.

Q: Well, probably the other part of it is there's a great psychological satisfaction in being able to apply and use their scientific expertise.

Captain Merrill: Absolutely. In the first six months that they were over here, they were not really used intelligently, to my way of thinking.

Q: But that's understandable.

Captain Merrill: It's understandable. We had just finished a war with them and, as a nation, we weren't too happy with them.

Q: What was your relationship with Truax and his operation?

Captain Merrill: Truax was a rocket expert from beginning to end. He had very capable people, and all I did was keep track of what he was doing and what he needed. He reported and, as far as I know, he was happy with the arrangement. He was very self-sufficient, because he was the officer-in-charge of a small unit in Annapolis. He had contacts in the rocket scientist community, a closed group, in many ways. In those days there was relatively little liquid propellant work going on within the Navy.

Q: Well, he'd had ties to Dr. Goddard, hadn't he?[*]

Captain Merrill: He did indeed. Of course, Goddard was one of the best rocket designers of his time. At Point Mugu he and Truax didn't work directly together.

Q: Well, Truax was sort of a disciple, wasn't he?

Captain Merrill: Right. But then Truax began to get into jet engines, small turbojets for example. Goddard was more the scientist type. He wanted to get into astronautics, so to speak. But they had a close relationship, no question about it.

Q: What were some of the applications of Truax's work that you saw?

Captain Merrill: If you remember, I talked about the Gorgon series. They were some of the early World War II prototypes. He supplied the rocket motors for the rocket versions. Each missile itself was done by some contractor, but Truax was given technical cognizance of the rocket. He actually built the first few rockets. Later we got into versions of Gorgon that used turbojets, and there we used an industrial company for the jet engine. Truax took

---

[*] Robert H. Goddard (1882-1945) was a noted American physicist. From the 1930s onward he was involved in research for using rockets to reach high altitudes.

technical cognizance of such missiles when they came to Point Mugu. Of course, the Gorgons were treated just like the other missiles.

Q: Well, you talked about your role not being development per se. Was that done at China Lake and you tested their products?*

Captain Merrill: No, most of the missiles we tested were developed under BuAer or Air Force contracts. China Lake's famed Sidewinder was both developed and tested there.†

We had quite a bit of cooperation, incidentally, with China Lake in those days, because they were further advanced than we were in missile testing, especially in the rocket side of the business.

Q: Well, I'm trying to differentiate. What was your role vis-à-vis China Lake's? How did they differ?

Captain Merrill: The main difference really was that China Lake was a creature of the Bureau of Ordnance, and we were a creature of the Bureau of Aeronautics. We got our money, our direction, our missiles and everything else from the Bureau of Aeronautics, China Lake got theirs from the Bureau of Ordnance.

There was a basic difference in their missions insofar as air-launched guided missiles were concerned. Under BuOrd, China Lake was charged both to develop and test missiles, while Point Mugu tested and evaluated but did not develop them; this is still true today. BuOrd felt that its civilian engineers and scientists must be allowed to develop missiles, notwithstanding any conflict of interest when China Lake tests its own missiles. The Sidewinder's success seems to bear out this policy. BuAer feared this conflict of interest, not only within Point Mugu but also with the defense industry. It preferred to rely on industry for its missiles and views in-house development as diversionary. Personally, I am

---

* China Lake is another name for the Naval Ordnance Test Station at Inyokern, California.
† Sidewinder is an air-to-air infrared-homing missile with a speed of approximately Mach 2.5. It has been operational, in various forms, since 1956.

aligned to BuAer's policy and believe it will prevail, now that both institutions are under one command. During the post-Cold War downsizing, there has been bitter undercover competition between the two because of their overlapping missions. This competition has enveloped the two communities which depend heavily on their payrolls.

Q: Well, there was a turf fight between those bureaus for a number of years over where the guided missile really belonged.

Captain Merrill: True. I guess I was part of it. It never really could be described as a turf fight, though. It was a competition; I'll put it that way. Del Fahrney, for example, was the first contestant from the Bureau of Aeronautics side. Yet he had a very good friend, a Captain Dundas Tucker, as his counterpart in the Bureau of Ordnance. They talked openly together; they never hid any information or did anything out of line. They both were busy as all get out, just working for their bureaus. But still there was competition between them.

For example, the Bureau of Aeronautics insisted on calling guided missiles "pilotless aircraft." [Laughter] It was just silly, in retrospect. But the underlying reason was that you had two power bases in the two bureaus, and they didn't want any infringement of their territories. Well, the only thing that they could fall back on was their past histories. Aircraft had pilots in them, according to the Bureau of Aeronautics, but then this rare weapon breed came along later that could only be called pilotless aircraft. Kind of funny when you think about it. BuOrd called them "guided bombs" for a while until the whole world settled on "guided missiles" and usage overtook both bureaus.

Q: Well, those two bureaus merged in 1959, and I understood one of the reasons was this competition, or whatever word you want to use.[*]

---

[*] Effective 1 December 1959, the Bureau of Aeronautics was merged with the Bureau of Ordnance. The new organization was known as the Bureau of Naval Weapons. The first chief of the combined bureau was Rear Admiral Paul D. Stroop, USN. His oral history is in the Naval Institute collection.

Captain Merrill: The merger made sense. At the time I kept asking myself--did the competition create waste, duplication of effort, and all that kind of thing?

Q: What was your answer when you asked yourself that question?

Captain Merrill: I don't think so. There was some overlap; I'll admit to that. We, for example, in the Bureau of Aeronautics had quite a few missiles that were rocket propelled, But the rocket itself is not a piece of ordnance, unless you put a bomb on it. So you got into all these discussions about what's a rocket, what's a bomb, which bureau should have it and all that. But in spite of all this, the weapons that finally got into the air and got tested and either turned down or accepted, probably were unhampered by such competition.

We were at war, and the pilots didn't give a hoot that Sidewinder came from BuOrd's China Lake and during the Cold War the submariners felt the same about BuAer's Regulus.

Q: Well, and if you make a comparison to the aircraft industry, the practice then was to have several commercial companies work on competitors for the same job.

Captain Merrill: Exactly. They'd compete for a big contract and that, of course, is the pattern today.

Q: Well, there are so many mergers, though, there won't be many competitors left.

Captain Merrill: That's true; the economics of downsizing is behind that trend. [Laughter]

Q: What was Fahrney's role during this period in the late '40s, when you were out at Point Mugu?

Captain Merrill: Well, he had been assigned to the Pacific area while I was still in Washington, and he went out there in a logistics command. In other words, he was in charge of a number of forward air bases and one thing or another for fleet support. In retrospect, I think he did less for the Navy being sent out there than he was already doing back at the Bureau of Aeronautics. But his career track, as seen by the Bureau of Naval Personnel and fellow officers on promotion selection boards, demanded that he have a variety of duty assignments on his record.

Q: Especially in the combat area.

Captain Merrill: Exactly, those old traditions hung in there for an awful long time. The specialists, AEDOs in Fahrney's and my case, deliberately chose a handicap from a promotion point of view.

Q: Well, that was much more true then than it is now.

Captain Merrill: Sure, you can even be a woman and get promoted today.

Q: Well, the irony is that he went out there to get that ticket punched, and then he didn't get selected for admiral anyway.

Captain Merrill: True enough. He wasn't ambitious for rank, but he wanted to be recognized as a real leader in his field, Today he is recognized as the "Father of Navy Guided Missiles." Of course, he didn't get selected for flag rank, and that probably was a disappointment to him.[*]

Q: What did he do then after the war and while you were in this testing program?

---

[*] When Fahrney retired from active service in November 1950, he received a "tombstone promotion" to the rank of rear admiral. Essentially, this was an honorary title, based on receiving a combat award during his time in the war zone. His final tour of duty, interestingly, was at Point Mugu, where he served as Commander Naval Air Missile Test Center from August 1949 to October 1950.

Captain Merrill: He relieved me. He came back from the Pacific and took over the same job that he left before. But in the meantime, the size of the programs had grown quite a bit.

Q: So he went back to BuAer.

Captain Merrill: Yes, as a captain, and it was a blessing that he did.

Q: Well, a very happy situation for you.

Captain Merrill: We had a wonderful relationship. I mentioned to you how he we fashioned this program of study contracts, many of which evolved into guided missiles under his management. It was a generic thing for the Navy.

Q: Do you remember any specific ways in which he was able to be helpful from his end?

Captain Merrill: At Point Mugu we got practically all of our projects from him and the BuAer divisions supporting him as a "class desk" officer. The latter were associated with components, for example, in the field of guidance or propulsion. Each division allotted funds to do its projects. Of course, Fahrney funded all missile test and evaluation projects. So I never felt underfunded for that reason.

Q: Well, let me ask your opinion on BuAer's interest and vision on guided missiles in the late '40s. Do you think it was more active because Fahrney was there with his background and enthusiasm?

Captain Merrill: Yes, I do think so. But, on the other hand, there was a lot of BuAer backing that arose from the fact that it was downsizing and was looking for something new to fill the vacuum. BuAer's visionaries, mostly the technical elements, had been busy developing the aircraft and their supporting hardware. Now they saw guided missiles as a way to fill that vacuum. Ultimately they sold that idea all the way up to and including Congress.

Q: Well, I'm just wondering, if this was the inevitable next step anyway regardless of whether Fahrney was there.

Captain Merrill: I think it probably was inevitable, but Fahrney speeded the process, because he had a master plan in the form of the contracts for preliminary designs.

Q: Well, if we could draw a parallel to something that was happening at the same time, that was the development of the nuclear power and the enormous drive that Rickover put into it during that period.[*]

Captain Merrill: Exactly, a very good analogy.

Q: Was the Loon the main project you were working on during your tenure there?

Captain Merrill: As far as flight testing is concerned, yes, certainly in the first couple of years. Although my time and efforts became more and more directed toward planning and getting the technical organization staffed and under way. It was probably a blessing that we didn't have any more missiles to test during the first two years. When the missiles that came out of the earliest contracts finally arrived on the scene--the Lark and the Sparrow for example--we had better instrumentation and lab equipment to test them.

We knew what was coming and when it was coming, so we had to figure out what kind of buildings we were going to house things in, what kinds of support aircraft we needed, and what targets we had to build or deploy. Control of flight tests had to be

---

[*] Then-Captain Hyman G. Rickover, USN, was considered the father of the nuclear Navy. He ran the Navy's nuclear-power program for many years, eventually leaving active duty in 1982 with the rank of four-star admiral on the retired list.

delegated to free the more experienced officers for planning. Much of this time was allotted to the architectural contractor, in defining what our requirements were.

Q: Well, how much can you tell me about the specifics of that planning?

Captain Merrill: Certainly the first milestone in that planning was approval of the Point Mugu site by President Truman. This gave BuDocks access to funds already in the budget.* To us it said, "Well, we're no longer going to use Quonset huts and these clapboard buildings that came down to us from World War II. We're going to plan out a center, and we're going to build permanent stuff--a permanent airstrip long enough to do the job, for example."

The first step, of course, was to select an architectural engineering contractor, and that was the Parsons Aerojet Company. Under contract to the BuDocks, they did their preliminary design work right on site with us acting as BuAer's agent for requirements. They moved a team in--on the order of 20 people--and immediately did a lot of survey work. Then they considered our requirements and started creating drawings and plans.

The most important thing, I think, was the dialogue that we had with them almost continuously. Probably twice a week, we'd meet with them and review their work and make suggestions and so forth. A measure of the depth of the plan, perhaps, was our estimated cost of the ultimate installation, $50 million. I really thought that would probably do the Navy for the next 15 years. At the 50th anniversary I learned that the total investment is over $2 billion!

Obviously, we had no notion of how huge the institution would become. What plans have stood the test of time? The operations center, as we planned it, was pretty huge. Two buildings that now honor pioneers by bearing their names were not in the plan. However, the administration building is still in use, with Del Fahrney's name on it.

---

* BuDocks--Bureau of Yards and Docks, the organization that oversaw the Navy's physical plant ashore.

Q: Well, you're not a facilities engineer by training. Did you have some CEC officers to work with?*

Captain Merrill: Yes, we did. We had Commander Deane Carberry.[†] He was sent out by BuDocks, one of their ablest officers. He was the project manager of our planning, with inputs from me and others. Of course, he also managed the construction through to completion.

Q: Well, for one thing, you would need cost estimates for building the buildings and runways.

Captain Merrill: Yes, all that was a specialty on which the Bureau of Yards and Docks did a fine job.

Q: Who sold the package to Congress? Was that BuAer?

Captain Merrill: That was BuAer and BuDocks. BuDocks probably had the leadership position in it, and BuAer had technical cognizance; both administered the selling process but Commander John Leydon, under Fahrney, was the "political" leader. Practically speaking, John cultivated the politicians involved, the land owner, and officials in DoD and other armed services.[‡]

Let me tell a personal experience that upset John in his work. The family that owned most of the property to be acquired was a gentleman by the name of Jack Broome; I met with him during the 50th anniversary. Anyway, during the war Jack had patriotically leased the land to the government for use by the Seabees. I think it was for a dollar a year or something like that. It was not land that was useful for agriculture, commerce, or housing, so it wasn't a terrible hardship to him. But, still and all, it was his land, and he had

---

* CEC-Civil Engineer Corps.
[†] Commander Deane E. Carberry, CEC, USN.
[‡] DoD--Department of Defense, which came into being in 1947.

plans for using the lagoon as a big recreation center similar to Disneyland. So when he heard that the selection board had selected his land for a guided missile test site, he began to perk up his ears.

Q: Who wouldn't?

Captain Merrill: Sure. [Laughter] A relationship existed already between him and the Seabee officers since he's a very amenable, patriotic sort of a person. Just a few months after I moved down to Point Mugu, I received a request to take him on a tour to show him what we were doing. We were in the midst of planning the permanent center with Parsons Aerojet at the time. So, of course, I acted as his host and greeted him at the front gate. Here I noticed that he had two or three friends with him. Later they turned out to be his lawyers!

Q: [Laughter] He was a smart rich man.

Captain Merrill: Yes. [Laughter] I took them on a Jeep tour and talked openly about what we planned to do: where we would put our launching sites, where we would lay down the long runway extension, and what use we would make of Laguna Peak--all of which were on land he owned. I didn't realize it, but his friends were taking down mental notes all the time. We parted genially after the tour.

Unbeknownst to me but well known to John Leydon, Jack Broome had already established contacts in Washington whose task was to obtain information useful in the upcoming negotiations for sale of the land. Navy officials were treating them with guarded respect. So the Washington Navy was being legally coy while I was openly promoting community relations!

A few days later I received a telephone call from John Leydon. It seemed that negotiations had opened, and the Broome lawyers were distressingly well informed as to what the Navy planned. Not only that, but they also confessed their source of information. John said that the "top brass" were ticked off and that I was to distance myself from Jack

Broome until negotiations were complete. I felt quite stupid, even though my intentions were noble.

Q: You unwittingly strengthened Broome's hand.

Captain Merrill: [Laughter] Yes.

Q: Well, how did it wind up?

Captain Merrill: Well, I was told to keep my mouth shut, to all intents and purposes. [Laughter]

Q: But the cat was out of the bag then.

Captain Merrill: [Laughter] Yes, but from that point on, I was not part of the negotiations in any way, shape, or form. I don't know to this day what was paid for what, but it all came out fine.

Now he is one of the best friends of Point Mugu in the whole community. I particularly sought him out at the 50th anniversary. We spent some time talking about those times, and I could tell that we hit it off pretty well; he wasn't trying to fleece the government. He invited me to come out and visit him again, which I will if I last long enough,

Q: Had he made a fortune in another field?

Captain Merrill: I don't think so. He had made a very good living from agriculture. He has lots of orange orchards around his home, and seems comfortably off. But the value of the land ultimately will far exceed anything that he got out of the oranges and agriculture, I feel sure.

Q: So he was just lucky to own the right property.

Captain Merrill: [Laughter] Yes, thanks to his forbears.

Q: Then what did you have to do from a public relations standpoint? Maybe the community wouldn't be too thrilled by having these missiles flying around over their heads.

Captain Merrill: Strangely enough, the general public seemed oblivious to our flight tests, probably because we never experienced an impact on populated terrain. I told you about the time we flew a Loon over Santa Barbara. Captain Hatcher was then the commanding officer at the center, and I was down in the operations center. So I called him up and said "Captain, we have a problem." [Laughter] And I told him what was happening.

"Well, what can we do? He replied.

"We have no valid options. We have no radio link to the bird. We can't shoot it down, because we don't have anything to shoot it with; we just have to pray." Then I had an afterthought. "One thing we can do is to put a press release together, because people are going to hear the bird and get on the telephone. We don't know where it's going to come down, we better start thinking about that." [Laughter]

So he said, "All right, you come on up here. You can't do any more harm down there. We'll put a press release together." So we went to work while the Loon was still on its way. The press release told how we always have an escort fighter, but it had not been able to shoot down the missile, primarily because we didn't want to set any fires on Santa Cruz island. By this time operations control reported loss of radar contact over the sea, well beyond the Santa Barbara peninsula. Having run out of excuses, we ended with, "But at all times the missile was under close surveillance by a fast jet fighter." That was supposed to give the public a sense of assurance, I guess. That's all we could come up with, so we cranked out several copies and ordered up two coffees while we waited near a telephone.

Nobody ever called, and the press never found out about it! Talk about an anticlimax!

Q: So you didn't put out your press release.

Captain Merrill: We never issued the press release, but wondered if we were to be "interested parties" to a board of investigation. [Laughter]

Q: In terms of public relations, did you, for example, go out into the community and make speeches at Rotary Clubs or talk to the reporters about the role of the center?

Captain Merrill: I didn't personally do much of it; I can only remember one or two such sessions. But we had other people, administrative officers, particularly in the air station. Public relations was the air station's job, and they did quite a bit of it. I guess it was pretty effective, because we had friendly relations as far as I know.

Q: Well, it sounds as if the public's reaction was curiosity rather than animosity.

Captain Merrill: Exactly so. We had just won the war, and who was going to put us down for that? So it was a friendly relationship.

Q: Any other projects you remember from that time?

Captain Merrill: There were a fair number of occasions, when Gorgons were tested out over the range. Also, I think some of the first Lark tests were made while I was still there. These, in general, were successful in that they were done according to plan; no accidents, normal results, no failures, and so forth.

I might relate one anecdote that has some historical interest, if not value. One of our distinguished visitors had asked for a briefing on our plans for the permanent center. He was Dr. Vannevar Bush, President Truman's scientific adviser. He listened to what we had to say for about an hour or so. We showed him the kinds of missiles we were working with and a cross-section of missiles to come. Then we got into the facilities that we were going to build. These included wind tunnels, rocket test bays, much longer runways, briefing rooms, and military housing that might provoke a scientist to muse, "Okay, I suppose they have to have these amenities, but where are the scientific tools?"

As we got through briefing him, he looked around at us, seeing a bunch of young guys, would-be scientists, if you will. He said, "Gentlemen, I want to tell you something. When all these facilities are finally built, rigor mortis is going to set in. People are going to start sitting on their hands in those buildings. Mark my word." Well, we had no answer to that one.

What he was getting at, I guess, is that we were planning for facilities that were going to wind up in the hands of a bureaucracy versus the hands of true scientists, of which he was one. As I write this, some 50 years later, I do not believe rigor mortis infected Point Mugu

To illustrate, let me tell how we got our wind tunnel. Frequently we had to hang missiles or special-purpose packages on our aircraft. To do this safely one needs to avoid turbulence that might affect control of the aircraft or add excessive drag. During the war such testing was done by the University of Southern California (USC) in its wind tunnel.

After the war, USC chose to stop this service. Ralph Peterson learned of this and came up with the idea of Point Mugu acquiring the government-owned instrumentation and modeling equipment from USC. Then we had to find a source of power. This finally turned out to be the main propulsion boilers of a ship that survived the Bikini Lagoon hydrogen bomb test.[*]

That's a far cry from rigor mortis!

Q: Well, and you had a great deal of enthusiasm for what you were doing.

Captain Merrill: We did, and I think it remains today. The nature of missile testing is not boring, and it's competitive.

---

[*] In July 1946 a joint Army-Navy task force conducted tests at Bikini Atoll in the Marshall Islands to determine the effects of atomic bombs on moored warships. Along with an array of U.S. ships were captured German and Japanese warships.

Q: Was there a satisfaction in starting to develop some American missiles, as opposed to adapting a German one, such as the Loon?

Captain Merrill: Definitely. We could see that coming. Actually the Loon never did get to weapon status, but it was soon followed by Regulus, which was tested and deployed by some five submarines in the late 1950s and early 1960s. That made us feel that things were going as planned. This was an important aspect of naval history. Navy submarines made a transition from torpedo shooters to missile shooters as well. That's an important milestone.

Q: Of course, they had a long interruption when Regulus got canceled before Tomahawk came along.

Captain Merrill: Tomahawk came later, of course, but added the capability of pin-point delivery of both nuclear and TNT payloads. I understand the Regulus was phased out starting about 1962, anticipating a phase in of Polaris nuclear SSBNs. The deterrence power of both missiles--plus the Air Force's strategic bombers--is credited with the Russian back down from the Cuban Missile Crisis. And that, in turn, foreshadowed the end of the Cold War.

Q: And essentially Admiral Burke made the decision that to pay for Polaris, he had to get rid of Regulus and reluctantly did so.[*]

Captain Merrill: You're right about that; it was a good decision at the time. We were ahead of the Soviets with Polaris and stayed ahead. I think that was a big factor in the Cuban Missile Crisis coming out the way it did.

---

[*] Admiral Arleigh A. Burke, USN, served as Chief of Naval Operations from 17 August 1955 to 1 August 1961. His oral history recollections of Polaris are in a volume devoted to that subject in the Naval Institute collection.

Q: Well, you could argue also that's what led to the end of the Cold War, that we maintained that strong deterrent throughout.

Captain Merrill: Yes, I think so. I didn't recognize how things would go, even when I was participating in them, so to speak.

We should note that the Norton Sound was out there doing a lot of good work too. And that contributed to creating knowledgeable officers and enlisted men that knew the game. They, in turn, set up their own training and the whole thing kind of burgeoned out.

Norton Sound's history in missile testing needs to be touched upon.* I first heard about the ship when I was out at Point Mugu. I think the Bureau of Ordnance and forward thinkers in CNO were instrumental in having the ship modified for missile testing, presumably those developed by BuOrd.

Q: She was based at Port Hueneme, wasn't she?

Captain Merrill: Yes, she was, finally. But that's because I was instrumental in asking for it. I like to think that, anyway. I know I drafted a letter to the Chief of the Bureau of Aeronautics asking that it be home based there.

Q: Where was she before that?

Captain Merrill: Somewhere on the East Coast; I don't know. But the letter that I wrote arrived about the time the ship was coming out of the yard. I don't know the story from the point of view of what happened before then. But I do know we asked for it to be based at Port Hueneme. It came there ultimately and stayed, off and on, most of the time. It was able to go out and cruise with the fleet occasionally and help in its training,

---

* USS Norton Sound (AVM-1) was a seaplane tender converted for missile testing. For a pictorial history, see Norman Polmar, "USS Norton Sound: the Newest Old Ship," U.S. Naval Institute Proceedings, April 1979, pages 70-83.

While we're on this subject, the fact that submarines could base at Port Hueneme was a great convenience. It bore out the utility of that harbor, just as we'd hoped.

Q: Did you get involved in what I think was called Project Bumblebee, which was the surface-to-air family of missiles?

Captain Merrill: Only to a limited extent. I often heard of it. It seems to me Merle Tuve was one of the scientists involved in it. We had a working relationship, and I knew of it. Bumblebee was a good, solid program, as far as I could tell. Also it evolved into the primary ship-to-air missile for all naval vessels.

Q: Was that happening concurrently or later than you were at Point Mugu?

Captain Merrill: I think that the Bumblebee family was started probably when I was in the Bureau of Aeronautics, I really didn't know too much about it or get directly involved with it. However, I was aware that it competed with our Lark ship-to-air missiles. As I previously noted the Raytheon Company's Lark was the first ever to destroy a target drone, to my knowledge. However, Bumblebee was coming along fast and enjoyed strong support from BuOrd. It was supersonic, whereas Lark was subsonic. Eventually Bumblebee swept the field; it was probably inevitable.

Q: Why would that not fall under Point Mugu?

Captain Merrill: You have to remember that even after Point Mugu was designated as the focal point for missile testing, competitive facilities were already in existence. For example, the Bureau of Ordnance had a facility housed at an Air Force base at Cape Canaveral, Florida. Today it is NASA's Kennedy Space Center.[*] Bumblebee was probably tested there and also at Army facilities at White Sands, New Mexico.

---

[*] NASA--National Aeronautics and Space Administration.

In that time BuOrd was viewed by many as a fraternal organization, called the "gun club," that took care of its own. There was no such officer speciality as "ord only" corresponding to aeronautical engineering duty only (AEDO). Its weapon development talent was vested in line officers who rotated in and out of weapon development billets. Vice Admiral Savvy Sides and Captain Bowser Vieweg, both of whom I deeply admired, were examples.* Perhaps for this reason BuOrd managed to stay aloof from Point Mugu, at least during my tenure and later when I was the first technical director of Polaris, working under Captain Red Raborn--himself a gun clubber. I repeatedly tried to set up Polaris testing at Point Mugu but was not listened to.

The essence of it is that the missiles that wind up later at Point Mugu usually are major missiles that need the sea test range environment, especially in their later phases when ships become central to the operation. That's when they show up at Point Mugu, where sophisticated instrumentation, ships as needed, and inland mountains and deserts with diverse terrain and targets were available. Tomahawk did most of its testing there, for example.

Q: What precautions did you take when you were going to send a missile out to sea. Did you put out notices to mariners, or what have you?

Captain Merrill: Yes, we did. There's not much sea traffic on the Pacific coast, thank God. So it isn't too much of a problem. There are routine lines of communication to the seagoing community. Even the fishermen know when the Navy will be testing and where. Of course, AVR boats and utility aircraft patrol the problem areas and warn ships and pleasure craft that may be in danger. So I don't think it's much of a problem or an inconvenience to the shipping industry.

Q: I suspect you had a lot of cooperation from the defense contractors, because they had lost that big bubble of wartime business. Any cases you remember in particular?

---

* Rear Admiral John H. Sides, USN.

Captain Merrill: During my 1946-49 tenure, the missile contractors were beginning to supplement on-base work space with rented space in nearby communities and today such space seems still necessary. Personal ties developed between contractor and Navy employees and their families. The Cold War was heating up, and there was no thought of today's "downsizing." Consequently, defense industry cooperation was just fine, as were community relations.

Q: Did you have any direct contact with the West Coast defense industry?

Captain Merrill: Yes. I remember when the Lark testing program started. The Raytheon organization rented a building off the base. Because they had so much activity going on, they felt they needed their own building off the site, even though their missiles were fired at or off of Point Mugu. There were a number of defense industries that did that, mostly the larger ones such as Lockheed. There was also a lot of vehicular traffic between the defense industries in the San Francisco and Los Angeles basins and Point Mugu.

Sometimes the companies hosted social events, but most social contacts were person to person.

Q: Did you keep up your proficiency flying during this period?

Captain Merrill: I did, but to be honest about it, it was the only way I could keep that 50% bonus on my salary. [Laughter] There was little or no chance that I would be assigned to a combat-ready unit.

Q: Well, that pay made it worthwhile.

Captain Merrill: Yes, it was enjoyable and useful as well. It was a therapeutic change of pace, to coin a phrase. I had to fly four hours a month in those days. Occasionally I had some adrenaline-raising experiences. Like the time Commander Ham Hauck and I flew over the sea range to San Nicholas airstrip and later came back to find Point Mugu socked in. Fortunately, our SCR-584 was in operation so they did a successful GCA approach for us--the first ever for me.*

Q: Interesting job for a fire control radar.

Captain Merrill: Right. [Laughter] Improvisation, I guess.

Q: Well, did you get to sea at all during that era?

Captain Merrill: Only on AVR boats. Actually, the last sea duty I had was on the carrier Saratoga. After that I went into utility squadrons and from there to postgraduate school. I didn't have much time at sea in the Navy, relatively speaking. Probably that is why our family's recreation focused on sail boating, both during my naval service and thereafter in the defense industry.

Q: Are there any other things to put on the record about the Point Mugu years before we move on?

Captain Merrill: The target drones are, of course, a vital part of any ship-to air or air-to-air missile program. Simulation of an aircraft target is extremely important.

Until about 1939 or 1940, Navy ships were shooting only at sleeves towed by airplanes. I was in VJ-1, a utility squadron towing those sleeves, so I've had some firsthand experience of it. In those days, the battleships, for example, were highly competitive. They had a competitive scoring system going. As far as their antiaircraft effectiveness was concerned, they were being rated by the number of pieces of shrapnel that they put through those sleeves.

The rules for a firing run were explicit as to altitude, relative approach angle, air speed, etc. Maneuvers were prohibited, since the only effect of a turn was to slow the sleeve and head it downward. Normally we would drop the sleeve in the sea after one or

---

* GCA--ground-controlled approach.

more runs, and they'd send a boat out to get it and count the hits. They were happy with their scores, especially if they won the "meat ball" flag. The total effect was a false and dangerous level of self confidence. [Laughter] They didn't want their scores to be lowered by any artificial trumpery, so to speak.

Q: Any artificial reality.

Captain Merrill: [Laughter] Yes, but at least they set the stage for Del Fahrney and his target drone project. Bobby Jones and his VJ-3 squadron came down to Guantanamo Bay while I was down there doing this towing. But they were so shrouded in secrecy that they were stationed across the main entrance channel of Guantanamo Bay. At first, I didn't even know what they were doing. But every once in a while I'd meet Bobby Jones in the officers' club, and he would tell me about some of the firing runs the battleships made against the drones. Rarely were they anything but highly unsuccessful.

Finally, the word began getting back to Washington. This, of course, was prior to World War II, and it was a godsend that this shock wave hit the Navy at that time. BuOrd accelerated all their developments that might improve AA defenses, especially the proximity fuze. But that's a separate story.

That's when the target drones first showed their importance to the Navy, and it never diminished as missiles superseded guns in ships and aircraft. In the Special Design Branch target drones began to simulate aircraft more faithfully. They also acquired on-board instrumentation for analyzing each firing run.

A whole industry grew up around target drones. A typical example is the Radio Plane Company, where Marilyn Monroe was said to have met President Kennedy. Previously I told of how my brother-in-law, Mel Tuttle, reported to SWTTEU in Traverse City, Michigan, and became project officer for small target drones of which Radio Plane's TDD-1 was the first. Ultimately he was mustered out, went to Radio Plane, and became one of their vice presidents.

By war's end, more sophisticated and costly small drones were being procured by BuAer from Radio Plane and other suppliers. When you buy them in the thousands, that makes for a pretty profitable industry. Point Mugu helped these suppliers improve their product lines.

Q: Were you working with these manufacturers?

Captain Merrill: We, ourselves, didn't contract for them; the Bureau of Aeronautics did.

Q: In what ways did you help them?

Captain Merrill: In operational and technical ways. For example, we showed them how they could work more efficiently when controlled with a ship's fire control radar, like the SCR-584. When a ship is firing at a small target drone, you want to start the firing run at a certain bearing and distance away, a certain altitude and at a certain time. We simulated that at Point Mugu, and the fleet improved it as standard operating doctrine. That's just an example.

Q: Well, wasn't there also a program of using surplus airplanes like F6Fs as target drones?

Captain Merrill: Yes, there was a lot of that. I don't know how they made their determinations as to type and numbers of aircraft conversions. But, of course, the surplus aircraft were always one generation short on performance. Also surplus aircraft, being old and decrepit, so to speak, were a maintenance nuisance. So conversions had their shortcomings. Whether to use conversions or manufactured target drones boils down to an economics contest between the two types. I don't know what today's status is.

Q: That I don't know. Teledyne Ryan became another one in that field.

Captain Merrill: Right, probably the leading supplier.

Q: Were they part of the picture back then?

Captain Merrill: I think Ryan got into it shortly after the war, before they merged with Teledyne. Ryan originated down in San Diego and got into it just after the war, via the Bureau of Aeronautics, of course.

Q: And they built the Spirit of St. Louis years before that.*

Captain Merrill: Yes, there's always a history in a company like that. The pioneers start it up, and then the megabucks guys acquire them.

Q: That's the pattern.

Captain Merrill: Yes.

Q: Well, anything more on Point Mugu before you move on?

Captain Merrill: Not that I can think of.

Q: Where did you head from there?

Captain Merrill: Well, I was detailed into several jobs that were routine, unexciting, and devoid of historical value. The detailers didn't know what to do with me after I had finished up almost four years at Point Mugu. So they did with me like they did with Fahrney, they sent me back to the same place in BuAer. [Laughter]

During the intervening four years, the Marine officers had been promoted a lot faster than contemporary naval officers, thanks to the war. So a Marine colonel was heading up my wartime organization--the Pilotless Aircraft Division, I think they called it. I thought I was coming back to take over the same job I had when I left. But meantime the Marine had

---

* Spirit of St. Louis was the plane Charles Lindbergh flew in his history-making crossing of the Atlantic in 1927.

moved in and he was senior to me and had squatter's rights. So we made the best of the situation, and I started working as a sort of adviser to him. He was a personable and competent officer whose name I can't recall.

Then some detailer realized that my training was in electronics, and therefore I probably ought to be in an electronics billet. So they moved me within the Bureau of Aeronautics to work under Commander Victor Soucek, a program manager in the electronics division, the guy that managed the money for their projects.[*] This preserved the sanctity of his seniority, but that was not a very satisfying job.

Several months went by, and then the person who headed up the Electronics Laboratory at Johnsville, Pennsylvania, moved on, so I was transferred up there. I spent a year and a half at Johnsville shepherding a few developments and considerable testing of industrial products. During this tour I was sent to Harvard University to attend its advanced management program, a three-month mind-stretcher which came in handy for the next job.

I was really not challenged by any of these post-Mugu duty assignments, because I was moving from one place to another and not in charge of any of them except the lab at Johnsville. I could have stayed and been comfortable there, but I certainly was ripe for a challenge.

Meantime, high-voltage things were happening down in Washington, leading to what came to be called the Polaris program. The President's scientific adviser convinced him to issue a top-priority task to the Navy: develop a submarine-launched nuclear ballistic missile. Rear Admiral Red Raborn, whose acquaintance I had made when I was down in BuAer and later at Point Mugu, was named director of the Special Projects Office, reporting directly to CNO. He wanted me as technical director, and I reported aboard a few days later. I had to leave my family in Doylestown, Pennsylvania, because the kids were in school and I was about to tackle the Navy's top-priority project

Q: Well, any specifics to remember about your time at Johnsville?

---

[*] Commander Victor H. Soucek, USN.

Captain Merrill: Only the time my son threw a bomb through a greenhouse roof. But maybe we should not put that in.

Q: I think the statute of limitations has expired by now.

Captain Merrill: Sure, why not?

Q: How did he make a bomb?

Captain Merrill: I guess he was 16 or 17 at this time, in high school up there in Doylestown. He was an avid Explorer Boy Scout, and one evening they were in the scoutmaster's apartment. They finished their meeting, and the scoutmaster had to go somewhere else. He said, "Well, you guys are welcome to stay here, but at 10:00 P.M. you've got to get out and go home."

Well, it was about 9:00 P.M., and they got to talking amongst themselves. In the nearby community there was a greenhouse whose owners were not very well liked; the feeling was mutual. So they thought up the idea of crafting a bomb and throwing it through the roof of the greenhouse.

First they found a small pickle jar big enough to take the contents of several shotgun shells belonging to the scoutmaster. Then they filled the jar with pellets and powder from the shells. Then they took a piece of yarn and soaked it in some flammable oil to act as a fuse through a hole in the lid. At this point they found out that they had some empty space under the lid; someone said, "No problem, just get a piece of scrap paper and pack it down on top of the powder. Then we'll screw the lid on." So somebody retrieved a piece of paper from a trash basket, crumpled it up, and packed it carefully around the base of the fuse. Several voices approved, "Cool, Dudes."

Q: Did they also put the pellets from the shotgun shells in the jar?

Captain Merrill: You bet! After they crafted the bomb they said, "Well, I wonder who's going to throw this." They drew lots, and my eldest son, of course, drew the short string. So off they went in the dark of night, to the greenhouse a few blocks away. Andy lit the string and threw. The fuse sparkled as it arced through the dark sky. Soon it crashed through the glass roof with a great clatter and fell down inside the greenhouse. Suddenly they recognized what they'd done and scrambled for home.

Of course, the owner of the greenhouse, who lived right next to it, heard the clatter and went roaring to the scene. He found the glass jar on the floor with a piece of yarn hanging out of it. The fuse had ceased burning, thanks be to God!

Of course, he called the police They arrived in the midst of flashing lights and roaring sirens, took the bomb to headquarters, and carefully examined it. Finally, they got to the stage where they unscrewed the lid and took the paper out. What was typed on the paper but a list of all the scouts by names! [Laughter]

About 11:00 that night I got a call from the police, as did the fathers of the other five or six scouts, to come down to headquarters; our sons were in custody. They had been rounded them up in various places in the community. All the fathers and the scoutmaster went down; all were soundly lectured and released on their own cognizance.

I felt very sorry for the greenhouse owner, but the scoutmaster put the offenders on call for service to the greenhouse for quite some time.

Q: Well, it was a lot happier outcome than if the thing had gone off.

Captain Merrill: Amen to that.

Q: What sort of work were you involved in during that period?

Captain Merrill: It was pretty routine. We had electronic projects--development of specialized equipment and testing of electronics products. The lab was focused on piloted aircraft emerging from World War II.

Q: Avionics?

Captain Merrill: Yes it was really an avionics lab, and the focus was not on development so much as it was on testing defense industry avionics. It had been doing that for at least four or five years, all during the war. So it was an ongoing, fairly routine operation.

Q: Well, wasn't it sort of a subcommand under the Naval Aircraft Factory?

Captain Merrill: No, it was created early in the war and named the Naval Air Material Center. However, its seed staff came from the Naval Aircraft Factory.

Q: I see.

Captain Merrill: Much of Fahrney's pilotless aircraft development, in the early years, was done at the Naval Aircraft Factory, It was usually an all-Navy development and became a habit. You have to remember, avionics in those days would consist of a radio voice transceiver, a ground beam receiver, and a Sperry autopilot for large aircraft. It became very evident, during the early years of the war, that the defense industry had to provide the avionics needed for naval aircraft.

BuAer's electronics division at first preferred to contract for avionics and supply them to aircraft companies as GFE (government-furnished equipment). This policy promoted standardization but inhibited integration of avionics into the total aircraft. In deference to this last point, aircraft contractors were sometimes allowed to subcontract for avionics tied closely into the dynamics of both missiles and aircraft. MAMC's electronics laboratory became a technical right arm for BuAer rather than an avionics developer.

Q: What about instruments for low-visibility flying? Was that part of it?

Captain Merrill: Yes, ground control approach equipment began to appear in the later war years, and there was an explosive increase in avionics ever since. This burdened BuAer's efforts to achieve low costs through standardization. They turned to Johnsville to write specifications to do this.

Personally, I don't think that the Navy should be very much into avionics development. The defense industry must be supported, not elbowed out by government competition

Q: Well, it's useful philosophical discussion, and essentially you're saying that the Navy's role should be to set the requirements and industry's to meet the requirements.

Captain Merrill: Exactly, I think an occasional bootleg development, like the one I talked about for close air support for the Marines, is justified by the fact that it's done fast and at low cost. It was a relatively simple development, and the tools were already there to put it together. When you have a situation like that, when the Navy can get in there and move fast, that's fine. But it doesn't happen very often.

Q: Well, essentially what I'm getting at is that from 1949, when you left Point Mugu, until 1956 when you went to Polaris, you didn't have either much challenge or much professional satisfaction.

Captain Merrill: Yes, I'm afraid that's true.

Q: Putting in time.

Captain Merrill: Let's say about four or five years.

Q: Any recollections of the chiefs of the Bureau of Aeronautics? Admiral Pride was one during that period, I remember.[*]

---

[*] Rear Admiral Alfred M. Pride, USN, served as Chief of the Bureau of Aeronautics from 1 May 1947 to 1 May 1951. His oral history is in the Naval Institute collection.

Captain Merrill: I remember Admiral Pride as an able officer but not an inspired or inspirational officer; solid New England stock.

Q: Very taciturn New Englander.

Captain Merrill: Yes. Compared to Red Raborn, under whom I served, a totally different personality, yet they both got results.

Q: Well, Pride was very good technically.

Captain Merrill: As chief he needed management skills more than technical.

Q: I mean, his service went back to Langley in the 1920s, when he devised arresting gear and so forth.

Captain Merrill: Right. Pride was an AEDO, wasn't he?

Q: No, he was a straight line officer. He later commanded the Seventh Fleet.

Captain Merrill: Including Admiral Towers, I would say that the BuAer chiefs I served under were quite competent persons. I had very little personal contact with them, because it was wartime and priority number one was strictly aircraft, as it should have been. So I was just an onion in the tomato patch with my target drones and pilotless aircraft.

Q: Well, BuAer really had more than just a technical role. It was involved in training and personnel assignments as well.

Captain Merrill: Yes. They also ran a massive aircraft maintenance program. They reviewed all aviator assignments. I know they had a big finger in that. BuAer was almost like a separate Navy when it came to aviators, aircraft, and their ancillary equipment.

Q: It was an empire.

Captain Merrill: I guess that's the way to put it.

Q: Well, your quiet period ended with the advent of Polaris. That had to have a great deal of challenge to it.

Captain Merrill: Oh, yes. However, let me make some preliminary remarks here. In a previous discussion of my experiences while serving in BuAer I told of witnessing several V-2 firings at Cuxhaven, Germany, in late 1945. On returning I wrote a report to CNO, via the Chief of BuAer, which recommended that the Navy set up a program, i.e. issue an operational requirement to develop ballistic guided missiles for firing from ships, including submarines, against strategic targets. This was favorably endorsed by the chief but was never acted on by CNO. The concept resurfaced in the mid-1950s. At first it was called the fleet ballistic missile and later evolved to Polaris and its progeny.

During the war I approached the Chief of ONR with a plan to use excess assault drone funds to continue his ballistic research missile which was well along as a research tool. Anticipating an operational requirement, this missile could yield much useful hands-on experience. Unfortunately, the chief of BuAer found a better use for the funds, which was understandable in view of the deafening silence from CNO on my report. Ten years later, during my two-year stint with Polaris, I often regretted this outcome. The four years I spent puttering around in BuAer and Johnsville could have been spent on ballistic missile development. Well, man proposes and God disposes.

Q: Was Raborn aware of your letter?

Captain Merrill: No, I wrote the letter to CNO in 1946. I didn't join Raborn until '56.

Q: No, but you had said that you had an acquaintance with him in the meantime.

Captain Merrill: Oh, yes. We knew each other during the SATFOR years. I doubt if he even knew that I wrote such a letter.

Q: But he was aware of your technical capability.

Captain Merrill: Yes, he was aware of that, and that's why he selected me to be his technical director.

Q: Well, please proceed with that story.

Captain Merrill: Okay. As I have outlined, my first awareness of the creation of Raborn's Special Projects Office was simultaneous with my orders to get down there and work in it. There I was, up at Johnsville, out of the Washington stream of communications. Then the President directed a Navy top-priority development of a submarine launched, nuclear armed missile for use against strategic targets. Thereafter, Raborn was chosen as Director of the Special Projects Office (SPO). Shortly after that he asked that I be detailed down there as his technical director. That, of course, is what happened.

When I reported aboard, I found an embryonic organization, so to speak. I estimate there were ten officers and five civilians that Raborn had selected and brought in. They hadn't reached the point where they were organized. But they did have, in hand, directives from the Secretary of Defense as to cooperating with the Army in using its Jupiter ballistic missile.

I soon perceived a consensus within the technical staff and Raborn that Jupiter had features that virtually prohibited its use in submarines. It used liquid oxygen as part of its propellant. Once the missile was fueled, we faced the problem of disposing of oxygen bleeding within the submerged sub. In his 1972 oral history interview, Vice Admiral Raborn stated, "The thought of putting these missiles in the confined spaces of a submarine under the water, would make an internal combustion engine of the whole submarine." Next, because the payload always determines the size and weight of a missile, Jupiter was too large to house, let alone launch from our largest sub. Finally, its structure was too fragile to withstand the stresses expected in heavy seas.

Q. Why weren't these fatal defects recognized before you got the directive to use Jupiter?

Captain Merrill: I can only surmise, but one function of SecDef is to ensure that an expensive development in one service is not undertaken if the operational requirement can be met at less cost by a weapon already available in another service. We presumed that some competent organization had made such a technical evaluation of Jupiter and found it to be qualified. Who did the study? Was it von Braun's group? Lacking knowledge on the submarine environment, did "whoever" consult the Navy?

But I do know that SPO wasted many months trying to make Jupiter a feasible solution. Every conceptual analysis only reinforced our conviction that a solid-propellant missile was best for the Navy, but we lacked proof on two points: first, we wrongly assumed that we were stuck with Jupiter's warhead weight (about 1,500 pounds, as I remember). This translated to a missile at least as big as Jupiter. Second, the specific impulse of available solid propellants was not sufficient to overcome assumption one.

Q. Did you work with von Braun on this task?

Captain Merrill: Yes. We had numerous conferences with him and his staff, mostly in Huntsville, Alabama. No one could question his command of missile technology or his genuine desire to find solutions. He knew the political value of having Jupiter used by both the Navy and the Army and did not give up, even as he better understood the submarine environment. He was willing to beef up Jupiter's structure, even when the changes would delay his own program and shorten Jupiter's range.

I can even remember a tentative proposal that he made to us on an exploratory basis. He had his engineers draw sketches and plans for a huge barge that could be towed submerged by a submarine. The launchings would be made from the barge when surfaced in model one, and submerged in model two!

Chrysler also tried to sell Jupiter to the Navy. They staged several presentations which were quite professional from a marketing point of view but ineffectual to the hardheaded and technically competent SPO staff.

Q, How did SPO organize during this time?

Captain Merrill: Raborn, of course, was the director, and Captain J.B. Colwell was his deputy.[*] J.B. was acting as director of administration, and I was appointed technical director upon arrival. The three of us met one day to outline the desired organization chart. Administration was to handle budgets, personnel, housekeeping, and public affairs. The technical department was to have sections broken down by the missile and its subsystems, such as propulsion, guidance and warhead plus ancillary equipment or services such as launching, navigation, fire control, tests, training and ship liaison. There was also a section responsible for warhead liaison with the AEC.[†]

This organization proved valid for staffing purposes and operations with the Army, Navy, and organizations relating to Jupiter. It even survived when we finally shifted to Polaris.

Captain Levering Smith, a recognized expert in solid propellants, arrived shortly after me and was asked to head up the propulsion section. He was actually senior to me, but, to his credit, was content not to ask for my job, probably because he knew that moving us away from Jupiter to a new Polaris depended upon his functioning well in his solid propellant field. He succeeded me when I retired in 1957 and finally succeeded Raborn. We worked well together.

Other officers arrived who were the best the Navy had to offer, in my opinion. Bob Wertheim headed up warheads and ultimately became Director, SPO in its Trident era.[‡]

---

[*] Captain John B. Colwell, USN. The oral history of Colwell, who retired as a vice admiral, is in the Naval Institute collection.
[†] AEC--Atomic Energy Commission.
[‡] Lieutenant Robert H. Wertheim, USN. The oral history of Wertheim, who retired as a rear admiral, is in the Naval Institute collection.

Inevitably any organization evolves to fit the management style of its leader. Raborn described his style in these terms in his oral history, "Not being burdened with a great deal of knowledge about anything, I just depend upon a lot of people to do the work for me. I would never do anything if I could get somebody else to do it because, one, the other fellow probably knew how to do the job far better than I, and two, it gave me time to do the things that only I could do. It gave me time to find the soft spots in performance or in part of our military-industrial team or in protecting our political lines in Washington and go do something about them. My deputy ran my show. The deputy, the chief civilian and the technical director were known as the 'Board of Directors.' Do you think I attended the Board meetings? Hell, no! I didn't want to get into the minutiae."

This self-appraisal was honest and accurate. By using this management style, he achieved remarkable success in the Polaris and follow-on missile programs, all with top-priority Navy backing.

What "only he could do" was to use his sales and social skills and his Navy-wide top priority to "do something about the soft spots." The "something" usually required a major change, such as more money, fire a lagging contractor or subsidize a winner, prod another service, etc. Many of these required selling his need and persuading government or industrial officials in power to give up something in order to help him. If the official was in the Navy, the task was simpler because he had the backing of CNO and SecNav. If the official was in the executive branch of government or Congress, the task was harder.

In this process he realized, early on, the need for modern presentation and program management visual aides. So he established a Program Management Center, under GS-17 civilian Gordon Pehrson.[*] It featured a large conference room in which dozens of progress/milestone PERT charts were displayed on the walls.[†] Each Saturday morning officers representing all functions of the organization gathered to present progress and answer questions directed mostly at "soft spots." The same room served to brief VIPs

---

[*] The recollections of Gordon O. Pehrson are in the Naval Institute oral history volume on the Polaris program.
[†] PERT--Program Evaluation Review Technique, a system of milestones for tracking the progress of a program against its schedule.

ranging from senators and government bean counters to scientists, engineers, or top administrators Raborn was trying to hire.

My officers and I doubted the value of these Saturday morning meetings. Pehrson was known as "Omar, the chart maker," because his staff had to get the information needed for the charts from us only for us to see the same information on the walls the following Saturday. Once I convinced Raborn to use a weekday for a couple of months, but Saturdays were reinstated. However, I conceded the room's value for VIP briefings, and it was often from these VIPs that major "political" decisions flowed.

Q. What precipitated the shift from Jupiter to Polaris?

Captain Merrill: Two events triggered the shift. First, Atlantic Research Corporation, a contractor to ONR, was encouraged by Levering Smith to try a solid propellant mix with a greatly increased portion of powdered aluminum. It worked, yielding a specific impulse about equal to the liquid propellant used in Jupiter, with no apparent ill effects. Second, Dr. Edward Teller, speaking for the Atomic Energy Commission at ONR's NOBSKA advisory group, said essentially, "The Atomic Energy Commission can get you a warhead with a one-megaton yield for 600 pounds."

When I heard of this from our officer attendee, I felt he had found the key we needed to justify going ahead with Polaris, as it was later named. Raborn, I, Levering, and the warhead officer met the same day and agreed to go for it. The next step was, of course, a letter to the AEC asking confirmation of the statement made by Dr. Teller.[*] Meanwhile we arranged for the preliminary design of a missile using these gorgeous new parameters. Both were in hand within a week.

In his oral history, Raborn describes what happened when he presented his proposal at the top of the Pentagon: "I very proudly carried this over to Admiral Burke and the Secretary of the Navy, and then to Secretary of Defense Wilson. I contrasted it with the previous program which he had approved for us to go ahead and showed him a series of slides of what it would do for size and costs of the vessels, where we could use it and how

---

[*] AEC--Atomic Energy Commission.

we could use it in submarines. The last slides showed the contrast with the program he approved, how we could put it into submarines and how we could save upwards of $50,000,000.

"When I finished the presentation, the Secretary of Defense looked most appreciative and he said, 'Well, Admiral, you've shown me a lot of sexy slides this morning, but I tell you that last slide, where you showed that tremendous saving, was the sexiest of all.'

"In due time, he indicated that he would give his approval to the dissolution of our working partnership with the Army and to proceed on our own."

Q: Were there, at that point, any precedents for solid fuel missiles?

Captain Merrill: Oh, yes. The World War II JATO (jet-assisted takeoff boosters) were not rockets, but they pioneered solid propellant technology. Then you had the air-launched HVARs plus the Terrier and Tartar missiles.*

We envisaged Polaris, using the 600-pound warhead, having a height of 28 feet with a diameter of about four feet. This required a solid propellant package considerably larger than any then in use. Our propulsion contractor, Aerojet General, ultimately came through on that problem.

Q: Was Teller's contribution that he had made the warhead more compact and thus able to be carried in a smaller missile?

Captain Merrill: Definitely. As you know, he was the architect of the hydrogen bomb and knew, technically and management wise, what AEC had to do to achieve his parameters.

In retrospect I blame myself for not recognizing early on that AEC would have at least two years to reduce the Jupiter warhead's dimensions to those needed for Polaris. All

---

* HVAR--high-velocity aircraft rocket. Terrier and Tartar were two of the earliest surface-to-air missiles installed in U.S. Navy ships.

we needed immediately was assurance that the warhead would be there on time and dimensioned as promised.

Q: He gave you the assurance.

Captain Merrill: Yes, his stature and knowledge of the business were enough to get us out of the dilemma we were in. I don't know if even he realized it at the time. Is he still alive?

Q: Yes, as far as I know, he is.

Captain Merrill: Well, he sure ought to be credited for that.

Q: You have already covered Raborn's personality and working style. Can you elaborate on how that affected internal SPO day-to day operations?

Captain Merrill: Okay. Raborn was a superb salesman; that's the first thing to be said about him. He inspired confidence in superiors who had to make a judgment on him, whether he knew what he was talking about and could produce results as promised. It's those qualities that sold him to Admiral Burke, who was then CNO. The two were much alike in some ways. Raborn also had experience with the wartime missiles,

He had one other quality that was important; he could spot officers and civilians with the qualifications that he needed and recruit them into SPO-people like Levering Smith, Bob Wertheim, Gordon Pehrson, Deke Ela, etc.* The quality I most appreciated was full delegation to me for all technical aspects of our day-to-day operations.

On the downside, I feel he demanded personal sacrifices as to overtime, excessive travel, and immediate attention to problems of dubious priority.

I retired in 1957 after 28 years of naval service. Frankly, I was "burned out." Like Levering, I seldom got "home" before 7:00 P.M., but Levering had a wife at home. Mine

---

* Commander Dennett K. Ela, USN, an engineering duty officer.

was in Doylestown, Pennsylvania, caring for our sons. The Saturday conferences usually kept me in Washington for most weekends. Running diarrhea was often with me.

When I finally decided to retire, I so informed the boss. He was aghast that I would not honor the Polaris top priority by staying put. I pointed out that Levering Smith was fully qualified to take over as technical director, which he did. After two or three sessions, Raborn finally accepted my decision, but I feel sure he ranked it with but after desertion! However, he never voiced his disapproval in public, and for this I was thankful.

We worked well together for almost two years. At the least, I helped free him from the Jupiter yoke, organized and jump-started the technical division and helped select the contractors who are the real heroes for Polaris going to sea in Khrushchev's face. For this, Raborn awarded me a Legion of Merit and wished me Godspeed on the last day of my naval service.

Q: How did the PERT System fit with technical operations?.

Captain Merrill: For many years the Navy and defense industry managed their operations using GANNT charts, a predecessor to the PERT System. It was simply a chart with a list of tasks which added up to the final product. Along each line were annotated milestones with target dates for their completion. These were adequate to serve as an agenda for staff management meetings. After Gordon Pehrson arrived and understood Raborn's need for a "dog and pony show" for sales purposes, he concluded that a sexier system was needed. A management contractor--Booz, Allen & Hamilton, I believe--devised the PERT charting system which Gordon used thereafter. It offered a chart where product subsystems were listed to the left in circles. Thence lines labeled, as activities or procedures, connected to other circles representing milestones. These, in turn, converged into a finished subsystem and ultimately the final product--Polaris in our case.

We paid the price for PERT in the technical division. For example, probably two hours of Mondays or Tuesdays were taken up by his chart makers coming in and saying to technical officers, "What am I going to put on my next chart for Saturday?" Then the officer, if he didn't know already, had to get on the phone and get the information. Thank

God, we didn't have to use code 800 numbers with today's interminable "press the number" options!

From my point of view, PERT was a diversion of the thinking hours that the technical people had available to them. Simple GANNT charts would have been better. Indirectly PERT also led to regular Saturday morning management review meetings which should have been held on work days.

The war was over, and my people felt their family and recreation time was being diverted to support chart making. I championed a change away from Saturdays, but Raborn allowed this for only a few weeks.

Q: Kind of busy work.

Captain Merrill: Yes. But then I have to be as honest as I can. Even if it was irritating to me and frustrating to many others, I have to admit that it usually sold visiting VIPs, even if they couldn't visualize much of the technical stuff. So it was a great sales tool, especially for Raborn's use.

Q: Well, it might have been a motivational tool also, to push people to get progress to show on the charts.

Captain Merrill: The movers and shakers in SPO didn't need any chart to inspire them. They were already going full steam ahead in the direction they had to go. A few words of approval from their superiors motivated them far more than anything on a PERT chart.

At one point Raborn contracted with a Mr. Clement H. Watson, a renowned Navy-industry consultant, on the "The Presentation of Ideas."[*] He was primarily a speech writer for Raborn and worked closely with Gordon Pehrson when graphic arts work, including charts, was needed. Here's what he said about PERT in his oral history: "It was the biggest problem in the weekly presentations made to the admiral because the charts were loaded with too much detail and there were usually too many charts. I fought a

---

[*] Watson's oral history is in the Naval Institute volume on Polaris.

valiant but losing battle to keep the charts simple and few in numbers. That's a war I never won!"

Levering Smith was more tolerant of PERT than I and may well have benefited from it after my departure. Tolerance and dedication to hard work were two of his strongest qualities. After all, he was tolerant of me, despite being two Naval Academy classes senior to me! One does not see this frequently in the Navy. He was also more tolerant of Raborn's demands for diverting technical officers to support his top-level sales pitches. Levering succeeded as a replacement of me, and later of Raborn as well. Who can argue with the success of Polaris?

Q: How was Raborn as an administrator?

Captain Merrill: He was simplistic but clever. His oral history describes instances of making decisions which should first have been cleared with the Secretary of the Navy or Defense. I suspect he acted deliberately, being well aware of his close ties to Admiral Burke and the value of his documented top priority within the Navy. He freely admitted his errors in each case and was duly forgiven.

I believe what I've said in the last few pages explains why Raborn succeeded in his SPO assignment.

Within SPO I do not give him high administrator marks. As his self-appraisal previously mentioned, he delegated authority but often surprised us with commitments made in top-level conferences which upset some apple carts internally. For example, recruiting persons whose places in the organization were vague, to say the least.

Q: Do you have an example of one of these cases where he made a decision half-cocked and somebody else had to clean it up?

Captain Merrill: I previously told of how Raborn recruited Clement Watson to be his speech writer and had a handshake deal before he discussed with Gordon Pehrson where he would be placed in the organization. Only after smoothing some ruffled feathers and convening a conference to deal with the question was it decided to put Watson under contract as a consultant, based primarily at home. This was not an optimum situation, as he finally spent most of his time in the Program Management Division doing some of the things Pehrson was already paid to do as a super grade (GS-17) civilian.

Another half-cocked decision was told by Raborn in his oral history. President Eisenhower asked for a tri-service briefing to his Security Council on their guided missile programs.[*] Raborn came away deservedly pleased with his own presentation and began to ruminate on other leaders who might help his cause by hearing the same story. Secretary of the Treasury Robert Anderson came to mind, because the program required him "to print" a lot of money. Once again enthusiasm out-raced protocol and he called Bob, a former Deputy SecDef.[†] Bob was pleased but requested a copy of the planned program in advance; this was arranged. The net effect was that the Secretary of the Treasury was going to see next year's multi-million dollar money request before the Secretary of Defense, Neil McElroy.[‡] Realizing this, Raborn entrusted a friend on SecDef's staff to explain the situation to his boss. He promised and then failed.

Two or three weeks later, Raborn accompanied SecDef on a trip to Lockheed in Sunnyvale, California. Raborn confessed all during an automobile ride from the airport. In Raborn's words, "I won't say he was angry, he certainly contained himself." After explaining his motives and apologizing, Raborn was forgiven. Here is his advice for posterity, "It behooves anyone trying to do a job of this kind to ensure that people who are going to pass on it are kept well informed on program status and plans."

Q: Well, you've called him a salesman. Would you call him an inspirational leader?

---

[*] Dwight D. Eisenhower served as President of the United States from 20 January 1953 to 20 January 1961.
[†] Robert B. Anderson served as Secretary of the Navy, 1953-54; Deputy Secretary of Defense, 1954-57; and Secretary of the Treasury, 1957-61.
[‡] Neil H. McElroy served as Secretary of Defense from 9 October 1957 to 1 December 1959.

Captain Merrill: My definition of "inspirational" is "one who generates in another a strong desire to follow his leadership in achieving success in an activity of his choosing." I have already declined to rate Raborn as an excellent administrator and cited examples as to why. Despite this, I rate him as inspirational because I followed his leadership to the best of my ability. To be less than excellent in a management skill is only human and must be worked around by an inspired subordinate.

Red Raborn inspired me by his dedication to duty; we both learned the importance of this at the Naval Academy. Also, I was inspired by his ability to sell the merits of Polaris as a deterrent in the Cold War. Even doubting Thomases were intimidated by the undeniable invulnerability of submerged ballistic missile subs to detection and attack.

Initially, the admirals under Admiral Burke deplored the diversion of resources from ongoing ships and weapons, not because of the Polaris concept but because its brand-new technology posed problems beyond any the Navy had faced before. They doubted submerged launching, precision underwater navigation, and inertial missile guidance to the accuracies required. Having in mind the enormous responsibility of pulling a Polaris trigger to start a nuclear war, they worried about White House-to-submerged-sub communications.

It inspired every listener to see Raborn get up and declare that all these things would be done, on time and within budget. They felt that he, Red Raborn, guaranteed it. Without question, this led to an inspired performance from his staff. Each time one of these milestones was achieved his credibility with skeptics went up. All the cats were in his bag when he issued a flamboyant press release, "Out of the Deep--on Target." At SPO Raborn was put into a very special program and was given top priority. No one argues with the results.

Q: He got high marks for working with Congress, for example.

Captain Merrill: Yes, He had a theater there that ran top-line monies. [Laughter]

Q: Well, turning to another individual, what are your recollections of von Braun?

Captain Merrill: I liked him very much. I first met him when we were directed to use Jupiter. He was a jovial fellow and very sound technically. He was a doctor in his profession and highly respected by all the Germans and Army personnel who worked for or with him.

The German missile expert that I worked with at Point Mugu, Dr. Herbert Wagner, was often referred to as a von Braun competitor in the World War II German hierarchy. Wagner's orientation was toward the German Air Force, as I understand it, and von Braun's was toward the Army. I never did talk in any depth with Wagner about his opinion of von Braun, but there certainly was mutual respect.

Q: Would you call von Braun a scientist with a creative mind?

Captain Merrill: Yes, I think he had that distinction. He could dream up ideas a mile a minute. I mentioned his concept of a towed barge to meet the Navy's need to launch Jupiter. That's creative thinking, albeit impractical. The term "scientist" does not really fit von Braun. He was more a "technical manager."

Q: Well, you said part of your job was organizing this staff. Could you discuss that, please?

Captain Merrill: I've explained that the technical staff was organized around the missile, its subsystems and submarine modifications to navigate, set up the missile's inertial guidance, and then launch it. What remains is to tell how this organization tied to our contractors; BuShips, which contracted for the subs; and AEC for the warhead. First off, let me describe the process of choosing contractors.

The standard procedure for doing this in this era was to invite competitive proposals in response to specifications for the aircraft, ship, guided missile, or what have you. In our case we lacked viable specs, because much of the required technology was yet to come. We also lacked time to do the paperwork involved with competitive proposals.

Consequently we were granted permission to use letter contracts, a procedure used only during wartime, as a general rule.

Probably the first and most important choice was Lockheed as the missile contractor. While at Point Mugu I had frequent dealings with Lockheed, especially through Vice President Gene Root.* I knew that they had deliberately emphasized aircraft over guided missiles during the war, because they rightly discerned that the war would be over before any missile could be developed and placed into large scale production. The assault drone proved this to be correct. Consequently, at war's end aircraft production and development of new models tapered off, leaving them with a reservoir of engineers skilled in the technologies common to both aircraft and missiles.

I made a trip to Lockheed to confer with Gene and several other executives as to Lockheed doing Polaris. They were enthusiastic and convinced me that they had the resources to do the job. I so reported to Raborn, who followed up with visits of his own, augmented by inspections from other SPO officers. Once we were all convinced, steps were taken to issue a letter contract using the cost plus fixed fee compensation protocol.

With variations, this procedure was followed with all the missile subsystem contractors, Lockheed being responsible for assuring that the subsystems were compatible with the missile. The warhead, of course, was supplied by AEC, again with Lockheed responsible for compatibility. BuShips was responsible for the sub; they used Electric Boat as their contractor.

Staffing SPO with officers and civilians went on simultaneously with jump-starting the contractors. I remember some section heads who participated in the selection of their contractors. Levering Smith chose Aerojet General for the solid propellant cartridge. My classmate Bill Keller helped BuShips start up Electric Boat, while Bob Wertheim worked with AEC on the warhead.† Deke Ela set up the launching system between Lockheed and Westinghouse. Meanwhile Gordon Pehrson fired up his management control center, and weekly conferences were soon being attended by contractor reps as well as SPO section

---

* L. Eugene Root was then the vice president and general manager of the Lockheed Missile Systems Division.
† Captain William W. Keller, USN, an engineering duty officer.

heads. All of this went from zero to functional in about three months. Quite an achievement, in retrospect.

With this experience under our belts, both Raborn and I came to believe that the competitive "cost-effective" procedures then in effect would be "cost-wasteful" in our case. Raborn may have lived with competitive contracting during the big-money phases of the Polaris program. It was a time when many subs and missiles were being built with money going out at better than a billion dollars a year. Here are a few abstracts from his oral history that express his disdain for the procurement procedures then in effect:

"The lessons of Polaris have certainly been lost on this country. It was a very successful program of major proportions--but now people seem to be more content to 'stooge' along following the many rules, feeling 'protected' while more bureaucrats write more rules to prevent mistakes as if there can ever be a substitute for common sense.

"There are . . . at least a million people in government whose jobs are built up on this bureaucracy of paper work and endless reviews of the program managers' work. Their jobs would be jeopardized if they stream-lined action taking in a more common sense, straight-forward way.

"Sure it was expensive, but we were spending at the rate of 1.2 billions of dollars a year and we produced the system three and a half years ahead of the original schedule So we saved six and a half or seven billion dollars. . . . The Country had a weapon system which it needed, when it needed it! How much is our Country's safety worth?"

Raborn ended his history with this punch line: "There's a lesson in this program for someone today. But can we turn back the tide of ever enlarging bureaucracy in military procurement?"

Q: Where were the offices that you were running this from? Was that in the old Main Navy building?

Captain Merrill: Yes, the World War II cardboard buildings on Constitution Avenue that housed the various bureaus. [Laughter] But it was okay; it didn't slow us down any.

Q: What kind of a work day did you have? You had the problem with Saturdays. What was it like during the week?

Captain Merrill: I commuted from an apartment to work, arriving at 0800 hours. First off, I unloaded my homework on my secretary and then tackled my in-box, looking for decisions that had to be made in order to get other people working. At 0900 hours I started with meetings; sometimes these took me to the end of work hours. Otherwise, I just played it by chance. I usually left about 1730 hours with a briefcase of homework. Raborn said he and Levering left at about 1900 hours. I estimate I was on the road about one day out of ten.

Q: Did you feel really depleted at the end of a day?

Captain Merrill: Pretty much. Fortunately, I had an understanding wife and my kids, even the one that threw the bomb through the greenhouse roof, were in schools, and were more or less self-sufficient. I left them up in Doylestown until they finished out the school year. But those were pretty tough months. It was no wonder I had running diarrhea. [Laughter]

Q: Well, it might have been helpful to have your family around just as a diversion for you.

Captain Merrill: Yes. I was also finishing up a series of books that I was editing on guided missile and space flight design. That took up any slack I had.

Q: Who published those books?

Captain Merrill: It was D. Van Nostrand. There were 13 books under the title <u>Principles of Guided Missile and Space Flight Design</u>. I contracted with the authors and edited all of them. I wrote part of the one covering operations research, the only subject I knew in depth. Somewhere along the line, I received the G. Edward Pendray Award for Excellence in Technical Literature from the American Rocket Society. Only two volumes remain in my custody, because I gave a complete set to the Point Mugu library. Incidentally, I also published a small book entitled <u>Defense Industry Management</u> with Exposition Press.

Q: Did you, in later years, feel any pangs of regret that you had not stayed through till the program was in the fleet?

Captain Merrill: To be honest about it, yes. I sometimes wondered how it would be like if I had stayed there and seen it through. My career in the outside world started with a bum decision. I went with Fairchild Aircraft as chief engineer of its Guided Missile Division on Long Island. Three weeks later the general manager was fired, ostensibly for losing a secret document when his car was stolen.

The only Fairchild defense contract of any magnitude was for an Army cruise missile, a competitor to Regulus. Its performance specs were way ahead of current technology. The Army was asking for everything that Regulus could do and then some.

The aircraft division was designing the missile and my division was supplying the avionics, mostly by subcontracts. The Army was unhappy with the avionics progress and forced Fairchild to make me personally the program manager for the program. The situation could only be termed a mess, but we had a breathing space of some three years in which I tried to beef up my engineering/management strength and get the avionics on track. A la Raborn, I persuaded Commander Ham Hauck to come aboard as chief engineer. The Army's confidence went up. Meanwhile our profit margin went down!

At this point, CEO Sherman Fairchild paid me a visit and said I'd better take a cut in salary. Even more important, I was to cut the engineering department by half. I told him that would wipe out the cruise missile contract. But Sherman, who was not famed as a long-term investor, remained firm and flew home. I felt the only way we could get out of our situation was not to cut the engineering department in half so I resigned, to emphasize the point. Shortly after that, they lost the contract and eventually went out of business. Ham Hauck went on to become general manager of Raytheon's Santa Barbara Branch.

I was naive in joining Fairchild. I should have recognized that they didn't have the management strength and resources to survive in the postwar defense industry. They were short term, bottom line oriented.

Shortly after that I went with what is now the Harris Corporation. I wound up as president of one of its companies, called PRD Electronics. That was satisfying to me. Among other things, we developed a computer-driven avionics test system for the Navy, which went on carriers to support aircraft. Through standardization of test equipment considerable compartment space was saved on carriers. I got a lot of satisfaction out of that, on behalf of the Navy. That was where I wound up my professional career in 1968. That is when I finally retired, cruised happily in the Caribbean, and started a second family.

Q: Please tell me about that.

Captain Merrill: It's part of my personal life, of course. My first wife and I were married for 42 years, so obviously we had a lot of faith in each other as I nursed guided missiles and helped raise three boys. I had four boys by her, one of whom died in infancy. The other three are still living and doing well. But all the time that I was involved in this hyperactivity, she carried on with the family. I was not nearly as close to my sons as I would like to have been. I began to appreciate that I missed something in that part of my life.

After I finally retired, my wife Mary Elizabeth and I did something which we always wanted to do. You see around me pictures of several sailboats that I owned over the years. Over there is an Alden schooner, which I took up to Canada a couple of times, and up and down the East Coast. Here is my favorite, <u>Mistress</u>. When I retired from Harris, Mary Elizabeth and I got on this boat and went down to the Caribbean, via the Inland Waterway. We sailed out the island chain and down as far as Tobago, off South America. When we returned to South Carolina, she suffered a flare up of latent beta thalassemia, a type of cancer of the blood for which there is no cure. She died there in 1977, a grievous loss to me. She was buried in the Naval Academy cemetery.

I spent about a year, beginning to realize that cruising around solo on a boat was not my cup of tea. It was great, very relaxing, very rewarding while I had her, but after her death I was lonely; my life had no social purpose.

To make a long story short, I remembered a young woman named Jane Anthonsen who had cruised on <u>Mistress</u>, along with her parents, before I retired. She had gone on to become a teacher, and I kept in touch with her. After Mary Elizabeth's death, I spent some time vegetating on the boat, occasionally cruising locally. Finally I decided it was time to make a change, so I contacted her mother and found Jane teaching in Kansas. The courtship was mercifully short, and I married her in Beaufort, South Carolina. I'm still married to her, nearly 20 years as of this writing.

Q: When did you get married?

Captain Merrill: We were married in 1978. We've had a great second marriage and a second family. Few men are as fortunate. My focus, of course, has been on my family activities now. But I've done a lot of volunteer computer work for schools and our church. Anne Arundel County named me as "An Outstanding Volunteer of the Year, 1993" for doing a pilot project on teaching homebound students using computer telecommunications and serving on its Citizens Computer Advisory Committee. That's the kind of life I've been leading.

Q: Well, in effect, you got a second chance with the two younger sons to do what you felt you should have done with the first group.

Captain Merrill: Right. I enjoy it no end.

Q: Please tell me about them.

Captain Merrill: Okay. There's a picture over there of them as little tykes. John is the oldest at 17. He goes to Broadneck Senior High School as a junior. I have been encouraging him to think about the Naval Academy, but the decision is his. His academic and activities records are impressive, so he should have plenty of good options. As you know, your own son is in the same high school.[*]

John plays the tuba in the marching band and orchestra. He also plays the piano fairly well, but he specializes in the tuba. He's an Eagle Scout with a penchant for hiking the Appalachian Trail and white water rafting. He's an outstanding young man. I'm very proud of him; I love him, and he loves me.

And then there's David, aged 14; he is steaming along in his brother's wake. He's the athlete and social star of the family. In the county's little league baseball infrastructure he has risen from a T-Ball whacker to all-star senior as a pitcher and first baseman. While at Severn School, David was on the academic honor roll and, probably more important, voted highest in his class for effort. He's a great hail-fellow, well-met type, a kind-hearted kid and a great comfort to his parents

Q: Well, I see there's a sign over there that says, "World's Greatest Dad," so they must appreciate you.

Captain Merrill: Yes, they do. Jane and I are blessed with our wonderful family. I call it my third job.

Q: Well, anything you might want to say about summing up all that we've talked about in the course of these interviews?

Captain Merrill: You are giving me a chance to pontificate, so here goes. There are some things that I would say up front for anybody that might be reading about my life. A Navy career can be a very rewarding experience. It can also be a stepping-stone into other rewarding careers. I think in my life I've proven that.

---

[*] The interviewer's son, Robert Stillwell, graduated from Broadneck High School in the spring of 1997, soon after this interview. In his senior year he was in a math class with John Merrill, then a junior.

The other thing is more philosophical. It is very important, early on, for people to get their priorities straight with their lives. What are you really trying to do in your life? Nobody's going to reform the world; Jesus came as close to it as anybody I know. So you've got to live in the world the way it is, and you've got to get satisfaction out of living in it or become a psychopath. Your satisfaction depends on what you do for the world and the people in it; it does not depend on achieving rank or wealth. To the young and inexperienced, this sounds trite but take it from this contented octogenarian, it is true.

Q: That's a wonderful philosophy.

Captain Merrill: Well, I didn't have it when I started. Aging sharpens your philosophical outlook.

Q: Well, I certainly thank you, Captain Merrill, for your contribution to the Naval Institute's oral history program. It's been enjoyable getting to know you and very worthwhile for history as well.

Captain Merrill: Thanks, Paul. Let me say that you certainly know your profession. I appreciate everything you've done.

Q: Thank you.

Appendixes To

Reminiscences of

Captain Grayson Merrill

U.S. Navy (Retired)

Submarines at the Pole

Captain Grayson Merrill, USN (Ret.)

"'Stand by to surface at the Pole,'" I announced over the loud speaker system. Swiftly preparations were made, and Shaffer turned to me with a smile, 'Ready to surface,' he said, 'at the Pole.'"

The first speaker was Jim Calvert, commanding officer of USS SKATE and author of a gripping adventure book, "Surface at the Pole." The second was Guy Shaffer, ship's diving officer and today my neighbor at the end of Martins Cove Road. The time was 17 March 1959 and the submarine was directly under a patch of relatively thin ice miraculously found at the North Pole.

This story stems from the author's conviction that there are many community residents in our country, for example the naval officers living in Martins Cove Farm near Annapolis, who have had linked experiences which would be of interest to Shipmate's readership. I decided to do a piece on RAdm. Guy Shaffer, USN (Ret.), '51 to test this premise. His wife, Marie, lent me a copy of Jim Calvert's book. I found it difficult to put down, a great "yarn" by any yardstick. I also found some places where Guy's career as a submariner and mine as a guided missile specialist converged to help the Navy gain a vital edge over the Soviets during the Cuban missile crisis. Here's the story, as extracted from my memory and Jim's book.

In 1945, a few weeks after the end of WW II, I was sent to Cuxhaven, Germany to join a group of allied officers and scientists to witness firings of V-2 missiles by impressed Germans from Peenemunde. After the firings the group gathered in a Bremen rathskeller for dinner, followed by a discussion of the implications of future long range ballistic missiles. A rumpled scientist, disguised as an Army colonel, summed up our feelings, "You young fellows must now go home and arrange to put this new weapon to work." His name was Theodore von Karman, famed head of Caltech's Jet Propulsion Laboratory.

I flew back to Washington and drafted a report to COMINCH, then FAdm. King, strongly recommending the development of ballistic missiles for launching from ships, including submarines. Not to my surprise, it disappeared in the bowels of the Pentagon without a trace!

Later I had a long lunch with my submariner Classmate, Worth Scanland. Catching my fever, he became an evangelist with his submariner friends to sell the idea that submarines, by virtue of their elusiveness when submerged, are the best launching sites for nuclear ballistic missiles. During the next two years, I wound up at the Naval Air Missile Test Center in California as Director of Tests and Worth showed up as skipper of USS CUSK, ready to shoot LOONS (a copy of the German buzz bomb) at a rock out in the Pacific.

Meanwhile, no new ballistic missile was being developed by the Navy. It took Dr. Edward Teller and President Eisenhower to light a fire under the Navy. In 1956 the President's National Scientific Advisory Group (under Teller) realized and articulated the great potential of submarine launched ballistic missiles. The President directed the Navy to proceed at "highest priority." RAdm. Red Raborn was named to do the job and he picked me as his first Technical Director in 1956. In July of 1960 USS GEORGE WASHINGTON successfully launched two POLARIS missiles while submerged off Cape Canaveral. In 1962 the Soviets decided to remove their nuclear missiles from Cuba. The threat of retaliation from POLARIS subs on patrol was certainly a contributing factor.

What does all this have to do with SKATE and Guy Shaffer? Guy graduated from the Naval Academy in 1951, from Submarine School in '53 and was detailed later to SKATE. She was the Navy's third nuclear sub, following in the wake of NAUTILUS. By this time the entire Navy had accepted the presidential priority embodied in the submarine-launched POLARIS missile. Much strategic and tactical thinking focused on the Arctic Ocean as an operating area, vis-a-vis the Soviet Union and China.

The Arctic ice pack is about ten feet thick on the average; a sub cannot hope to break through it unless it first locates a patch of thin ice big enough to hold the sub. Such "polynyas" exist, especially near the perimeters of the ice pack, but are fewer in the winter. When NAUTILUS passed under the North Pole in 1957 she was not equipped to surface in ice and had to settle for staying submerged. SKATE boasted an "ice machine," really a sonar pointing up, which yielded information on a polynya above. Other modifications protected her topsides from damage when rising through the ice. The limitations of both magnetic and gyro compasses near the pole were largely overcome by the sub's "inertial Navigation" equipment. Her nuclear power freed her from dependence on air for diesel engines or human breathing.

At last submarines were technologically ready to perform military missions in the Arctic Ocean. But it had to be demonstrated to the world.

Author Jim Calvert describes some of the history of pioneer subs in the Arctic. Novelist Jules Verne, of course, envisioned his NAUTILUS cruising, rather comfortably, under the ice pack; hence the name of our first nuclear sub. Sir Hubert Wilkins, in the 1930s, raised funds to buy an old and decrepit World War I sub from the US Navy which he refurbished and then deployed, trying to reach the North Pole in 1931. Repeated engine breakdowns left him calling for help in the mid Atlantic.

I was then in the battleship USS ARKANSAS, in company with WYOMING, as a Youngster. To the great relief of my shipmates enroute to Scotland and Denmark, WYOMING was directed to tow NAUTILUS to England. I recall the sad sight of a wallowing sub trying to acquire a towing hawser as we steamed east.

Not one to give up, Sir Hubert persevered and readied his sub for the Arctic. Some of his weary crew are suspected of sabotaging the stern diving planes; in any case they fell off. NAUTILUS pressed on to latitude 82 degrees and charged twice into the ice pack (with positive buoyancy!) in an effort to make their first dive. Suffering irreparable damage, Sir Hubert gave up, returned to Spitzbergen and deliberately sank the sub in a nearby deep fjord.

Quoting Jim Calvert, "Sir Hubert must truly have been, as his friends have often stated, a man who did not understand the meaning of fear. But the men associated with him did. Lacking the cohesive organization of a military ship and skippered by Danenhower, whose administration, in Wilkins' kindest understatement, '... was not always of a character conducive to maximum efficiency,' the men simply became frightened." More about Sir Hubert later.

Guy made two voyages to the Arctic in SKATE. Her (then) top secret operations order for the first voyage in August 1958 stated: "Depart New London and proceed to a point west of Spitzbergen, transiting via the Denmark Strait and the Norwegian Sea. When satisfied that conditions are correct, proceed under the arctic ice pack to the vicinity of the North Pole . . ." A list of missions included *"Develop techniques for surfacing in pack ice areas . . . all other missions are subordinate to this one . . . The military usefulness of an ocean area is dependent on at least periodic access to its surface."* Because of cold war tensions, skipper Jim Calvert was the only crew member to know that NAUTILUS would precede SKATE to the North Pole. The impact of Sputnik on world public opinion had to be countered. Thus NAUTILUS became the first sub under the pole, even though she was not equipped to surface there. Jim found it difficult to overcome the dip in crew morale when NAUTILUS' success broke in the news because, of course, they expected to be first. But they soon got busy with the untried art of surfacing in thin ice. The ice machine was the answer.

Under the ice pack, SKATE normally cruised at 16 knots and 400 feet depth, well below the deepest pressure ridges. The ice machine echoes told the depth under the ice and roughly how thick it was.

When hunting for a polynya, the sub came up just under the ice, using the periscope to look for higher light levels and ice machine echoes which indicated the thickness of the ice. The approximate boundaries of these "lakes" could also be estimated.

Once a suitable polynya was found, the sub was conned directly under it and stopped in a position for surfacing without striking the surrounding heavy ice. The final step was to surface vertically, much like a balloon, by carefully controlling the water ballast. These brand new maneuvers had to be "learned by doing" and laid heavy burdens on the navigator and the diving officer. By participation and tutelage, Guy learned these skills and was later named diving officer for the second voyage.

Unlike a diesel powered sub, SKATE faced a special hazard when operating deep within the ice pack. If the nuclear power failed, the relatively small battery would be required to restart the system. Otherwise surfacing under the ice was a very long shot indeed. Despite this, the skipper elected "to reach the Pole first, then experiment." Fortunately he was able to practice a vertical surfacing beforehand in a polynya well suited to the experiment.

"We moved slowly back and forth, plotting our position as we went and attempting to draw a picture of the opening. Finally we came to a stop beneath the center. I raised the periscope against the pressure of the sea. There was a huge jellyfish staring into the scope!"

This success and the contact with fresh air and arctic scenery buoyed the crew's spirits. They knew they could use these lakes to surface and to conduct military operations, if necessary. Proceeding submerged to the Pole would be duck soup! On 12 August SKATE passed underneath the northernmost part of our planet; every direction south!

After the inevitable "high fives" and other celebrations, Jim Calvert reopened his operations orders. "If the Pole is reached by the fourteenth of August you are authorized to proceed to the vicinity of Drifting Ice Station Alfa, attempt to communicate with its personnel and further, to attempt to surface near enough so that contact can be made." Alfa was a scientific observation village situated on a floating island of ice. It was supported by Air Force planes and personnel. Locating Alfa and surfacing nearby was chanceful amd dangerous. After leaving the Pole, SKATE surfaced awash in a dubious polynya long enough to send out a radio call which was answered by a Navy operator in Manila!

In a few hours Alfa replied, "Best estimate 85 north, 135 west. Many polynyas in vicinity but best within 50 yards of our main building." Final contact was made when SKATE heard the put-put noise of an outboard powered, rubber dinghy purposely stationed in the polynya.

A few days of R&R at Alfa Station relieved the crew of the tensions which went before. They set sail for Bergen, Norway, and a triumphant return to Boston knowing that they had succeeded in their mission. Later, at New London, Jim Calvert hosted Sir Hubert Wilkins on board SKATE. He died shortly thereafter.

When SKATE deployed from New London in March, 1959 on her second Arctic voyage, her ice fathometer was backed up by a protected but trainable television camera which helped in controlling the boat as she rose through relatively thin but still dangerous ice. In skipper Jim Calvert's words, "What the wealth of our country could do for us, it had done; the rest was up to us."

*The timing of the second voyage was deliberately chosen to test SKATE's ability to surface in the thicker ice of winter. After all, a nuclear ballistic missile which can't be fired in the Winter is not much of a deterrent. As the boat moved north beyond the Arctic Circle, the in*struments showed thicker and fewer polynyas than in Summer. However, a few long leads of ice, some three to six feet thick, were detected by dim daylight showing through to the T camera.

Calvert decided to try breaking through one lead as a necessary prelude to surfacing at the North Pole. He told Guy to "bring her up but take it easy." There was a sensation like that of being on an elevator stopped too quickly. They had not broken through and started to descend.

Calvert tried again. "We'll hit it again, harder this time." There was a sickening lurch as they hit—but now the television screen was filled with the image of splashing water and bits of shattered ice. They were through!

Days passed as they cruised north, finally reaching the North Pole where they searched again for a suitable ice lead. Miraculously a dog-legged lead showed up, barely wide enough to accommodate the sub. The first try at surfacing was aborted when they discovered that the ice was drifting on the water. They had to allow for this drift and still align the sub with the axis of the lead, not an easy task for a 3000 ton cigar, as likely to move up as down. But they did it!

"Stand by to surface at the Pole," Calvert announced over the speaker system. "Ready to surface," Shaffer replied, "at the Pole!" Finally SKATE lay on the surface—the first ship in history to sit at the very top of the world, which turned ponderously beneath.

A gale of wind was blowing and the restless ice was threatening to close in. Hastily preparations were made for a ceremony of commemoration to Sir Hubert Wilkins. Out on the ice burial party scattered his ashes to the wind. They quickly disappeared into the half darkness and swirling snow. Sir Hubert Wilkins had reached his final resting place. SKATE's mission was accomplished. What did it really mean?

In the arcane business of counterintelligence one enhances the deterrence value of a weapon system, POLARIS in this instance, by publicizing its invulnerability. NAUTILUS and SKATE proved that American ballistic missile subs could surface in polynyas to launch missiles against the Soviet Union. In the open ocean, sonobuoys dropped from aircraft are very effective in detecting submerged subs and attacking them. But the Arctic ice pack provides a shield against such ASW operations.

These facts were doubtless in the minds of Soviet officials when they decided to remove their missiles from Cuba in 1962 and may have contributed to the later dissolution of the Empire.

General Meeting,
Missile Technology
Historical Association
April 26, 1984.

The Birth and Boyhood of Point Mugu

The most valued relationship in my naval career was with Admiral Del Fahrney, the "father of naval guided missiles" (if anyone can be so named) and probably well known to all of you. At the end of World War II he relieved me as Director of BuAer's Pilotless Aircraft Division. In the turnover process he asked if I had kept a history of the Division's work and was obviously disappointed when I replied "no," followed by the usual excuses. Then he said, with understanding, "You fellows have been so busy making history that you've not had time to record it." I've never forgotten those words and their meaning has become more and more clear down through the years.

Probably most of us here tonight gave lip service, as students, to the notion that history is a valuable teacher. We memorized enough dates and causes of wars to get a passing grade and then rushed into the professional world to gain fame and fortune and reinvent the wheel. Most of us were also compartmentalized in bureaus, test stations, or companies involved in guided missile development. We must have done well, all-in-all, or our country today would not be in the forefront of missile technology. But now we have the time and maturity to look back and ask, "What the hell happened?"

If our Association can help answer this earthy question we can then turn to our youth and say, "Here's the real story of guided missiles in our Navy. You can learn very valuable lessons from it; how they were conceived, designed, tested, produced and used in the Fleet. These are the province of technology and operations. But of equal importance is how they were sometimes oversold, mismanaged and victimized by political in-fighting. These are the province of politics and bureaucracy.

It is only in recent years that historians have been able to crack the security barrier, with help from the Freedom of Information Act, and cull from government documents enough facts to give us a broad-based and accurate statement of what really happened.

Recently I had the privilege of reviewing the manuscript of a scholarly work by Dr. Derk Bruins on naval bombardment missile development through 1958. It is thoroughly researched and lucidly written with uncommon insight on both the scientific and political decisions of those years. For me it refreshed many dormant memories and made me realize what a broad scenario governed such programs as the rise and fall of REGULUS and the build-up of Point Mugu. I read it avidly, like a gripping novel, and I would guess that most of you will do likewise when it is published.

Tonight, however, I want to tread lightly and relate some of the events I remember about the birth and boyhood of Point Mugu. Please bear with occasional embellishment of a sea story and lack of accuracy due to a fading memory. There are many in the audience whose experiences overlap my own. Therefore I plan to take some of our allotted time for a floor discussion. So please line up some comments as I go along.

The need for a post-World War II naval guided missile range evolved from the wartime testing headaches of the Bureaus of Aeronautics and Ordnance. BAT was flight tested by a small unit based at Philadelphia against targets in New Jersey. NOTS Inyokern tested the ballistic rockets of those days and graduated to limited range guided missiles. The Assault Drone Program involved tests in Michigan, the Chesapeake and the South Pacific and finally vested in a Special Weapons Test and Evaluation Unit which became the nucleus for staffing Point Mugu.

In October of 1944 I drafted a letter which the Chief of BuAer signed out to CNO. It made a case for a naval missile test range and asked that a committee be established to survey possible sites and recommend the best. In January, 1945 it was approved and I found myself on tour with Chairman Bowser Vieweg and ten or so other members from other services. We visited and turned down such sites as Wallops Island, Roosevelt Roads and NAS Banana River (which later became the Atlantic Missile Range). Emphasizing technical requirements, we first chose a site at the northern apex of the Gulf of California--

firing down the Gulf. Sensing the political impracticability of this we nominated Point Mugu as a strong alternate. This, of course, was CNO's final choice.

Shortly after this I was detailed to witness some V-2 firings at Cuxhaven staged by the British and executed by Germans from Peenemunde. It reinforced, in my mind, the correctness of choosing Point Mugu. After the firings a small group of American observers gathered in a Bremen rathskeller to quaff beer and discuss what we had seen. A rumpled fake Army Colonel named Theodor von Karman summed up our feelings, "You young fellows must now go home and arrange to put these Germans to work. In the meantime build a test range for the missiles to come."

Almost 20 years later it can be said that Point Mugu has borne out the committee's judgements. The test range uses the beach or a nearby ship for launching, the trajectory is monitored by instrumentation on Laguna Peak and the Channel Islands. San Nicholas is useful for recovery. Port Hueneme has become a harbor for participating ships and the proximity of California industry has proven to be a great boon.

What we did not foresee is the advent of Vandenberg Air Force Base and the escalation of Point Mugu to be the Pacific Missile Range. We vaguely envisioned a long range trajectory southerly to such islands as Guadalupe and Clipperton, but it took the ICBMs to set up Kwajalein as a target and space flight to demand polar orbits.

Perhaps the first cruise missile to fly from the sea range over California terrain was a LOON which transited the Santa Barbara Peninsula about 1947. (This discounts an earlier LARK which circled the airstrip and plowed up some mud on base.) The LOON lost radio control soon after launch and turned slowly north over Santa Cruz Island where the escort fighter exhausted its ammunition in a futile effort to shoot it down. The horrified pilot reported the bird over the peninsula and entering a fog bank at about 2000 feet. Captain Hatcher called to remind me that the plan to acquire land for the permanent test center was then under attack in Washington by local citizens. We agreed that our best option was to prepare a well thought out press release. When last seen on radar the LOON had miraculously straightened out and was headed out to sea but we wondered how many farmers had heard the pulse jet engine and were calling the local newspapers. We were ready. The key phrase in the press release was, "The missile was, at all times, under surveillance by a fast jet fighter." The dreaded call never came.

If CNO's go-ahead decision marked Point Mugu's conception, its gestation began with the establishment of the Pilotless Aircraft Unit in 1945 at the nearly deserted and somewhat decrepit NAS Mojave with a rocket and LOON detachment at Point Mugu. Around 250 naval and civilian personnel were involved, mostly from units in Traverse City, Michigan and Annapolis. The key people and their organization are well covered in NAMTC's 1956 book "Ten Years of Progress" and, I'm told, in an updated history now in progress. So I'll stick to some personal experiences subsequent to my reporting aboard as Technical Director in early 1946.

Our test projects, in those days, involved the missiles left over from World War II. One example was a GLOMB or glider bomb which was towed to the target, released and guided by TV and radio control to impact on the target. One Gene Harris was charged with instrumenting the tests. He spray-painted a sand dune for a target and dug out a bunker some 100 yards away. From there he used a movie camera to film the incoming missile and a tape measure to get miss distance. I was somewhat shook up by this technique but he showed me calculations proving that he had a probability of less than 1 in 1000 of being hit so I let him continue. On the assault drones, however, I asked him to move his bunker farther away since each impact featured a large gasoline fireball.

Telemetry was not available to us, except for TV scanning of a missile's instrument panel, so we scrounged hungrily for ballistic cameras to correlate trajectories with radio commands. BuAer got us a few Askania Phototheodolites from a batch captured from the Germans. They arrived badly in need of overhaul. Having no optical facilities we turned to our colleagues at Inyokern for help. We should have realized that they were as hungry for Askanias as we were. Several months later we got them back in time to install them at Point Mugu. Meanwhile, at Point Mugu, Ali Baba (Bob Truax) and his forty thieves were liberating cement and steel from Seabees too busy mustering out to notice. Their liquid rockets appeared later in Gorgon missiles. Jack Schoenhair's gang was emplacing LOON launchers on the beach, together with a very temperamental powder catapult.

Another scrounging operation, which later paid big dividends, was the location and liberation of several SCR-584 radars. I'm vague on some of the details but I recollect they came one-by-one by truck from an Army depot near Sacramento driven by an heroic civilian engineer who masterminded the caper. He deserves a citation from the Historical Association. Maybe someone here tonight can furnish his name.

Scrounging World War II material was a vital factor in Point Mugu's boyhood. Shipboard search radars sprouted on Laguna Peak and on the islands and boilers from the Bikini-survivor carrier INDEPENDENCE powered a wind tunnel. Whatever became of the predecessor tunnel powered by some 16 Allison engines?

In retrospect, the work done by the people at Mojave and Point Mugu in the gestation period, that is the 9 months prior to commissioning NAMTC, was more in learning-by-doing and the emergence of a skilled technical and operating team than in the test results themselves. On October 1, 1946 the Center was commissioned and the hegira of parboiled workers and their families from Mojave to Point Mugu commenced. The boyhood era had arrived.

It was about this time that serious planning got underway on the facilities needed to expand the range for testing post World War II missiles, especially those in BuAer's program. A backward look at this program is timely.

Del Fahrney and I shared some convictions about what BuAer should do after the war:

1. Neither Allied nor Axis guided missiles had a decisive impact on the war's outcome.

2. There was a strong consensus, however, that guided missiles could greatly augment the Fleet's fighting capabilities.

3. The defense industry serving the Navy and our own personnel needed education on missile technology, especially the more advanced German concepts.

4. The advent of nuclear warheads gave missiles a destructive power which offset their complexity and expense; a marriage was inevitable.

5. Prospective tight budgets and a world-wide yearning for peace suggested that we had time to pause and think about missile specifications prior to their development.

We agreed that a broadly-based industrial study of missiles having potential to augment ship or aircraft firepower was the way to go. He nominated me to chair a BuAer committee to draft preliminary requirements for such missiles. In December of 1945 we submitted our "Study of the Requirements for Pilotless Aircraft for Fleet Use in 1950"; as I recall, it described some 16 missiles.

After its approval by CNO and SECNAV three months later, Del launched a vigorous program of many industrial contracts which, over the years, evolved into development of such missiles as REGULUS, RIGEL, BULLPUP and the SPARROW family.

The concurrency of the study contracts was a great help to us in formulating the test requirements of missiles to come and guiding Parsons-Aerojet in laying out the instrumentation sites and facilities of NAMTC.

In looking back, I believe the post-war study program was highly successful but boy were we wrong on the phrase "for Fleet Use in 1950"!

The year 1946 featured bitter inter-service cognizance battles in Washington. We were largely unaware of these and certainly did not realize that the very existence of Point Mugu was at stake. To quote from Dr. Bruins' manuscript, " . . . it seemed evident that the AAF was delaying action on JCS 1620 in an attempt to obtain primary and overall cognizance regarding guided missiles. At this very same time, General LeMay was leading the opposition to the GMC-JCS (Guided Missile Committee of the Joint Chief of Staff) recommendation that the Navy be permitted to build a missile test facility at Point Mugu, California."

Unaware of this hassle, I was detailed one day to brief Dr. Vannevar Bush on our operations and forward planning. As wartime Chief of the Joint Research and Development Board his voice was neutral but powerful in Washington but, to this day, I don't know whether he was evaluating us or just intellectually curious. Certainly he was close-mouthed, except for some penetrating questions. At the end of the briefing he remarked, "You people are doing lots of useful things with very little. After all these planned facilities are built, rigor mortis will set in. I've seen it happen before."

I concede his reference to one of the "Peter Principles" but I don't think it has happened at Point Mugu. In any case, Navy plans were not thwarted. The facilities came into being and obviously have contributed to the successes achieved here. Let me synopsize some of these.

As soon as the Air force was able to recover enough V-1 debris from the rubble of London, it hired Republic Aircraft to make some 1500 copies. A long war against Japan seemed inevitable and the V-1s were to be an Air Force contribution. Meantime our submariners were thinking about their role in the next war--with you know who.

One answer seemed to be submarine-launched SSMs for use against "Shore targets of naval interest." BuAer and CNO hatched up the LOON project as a learn-by-doing program, designed to bring submarines and missiles together. This it did, with the help of NAMTC. Over 100 missiles were fired from the beach or from CUSK, CARBONERO or NORTON SOUND at sea. The original unguided V-1s supplied by the AAF were equipped with aircraft beacons for radar tracking and radio control. Later refinements included control through radar signals and an automatic command computer. These evolved into the TROUNCE guidance system as applied to REGULUS.

Despite its inherent lack of reliability, LOON achieved some spectacular operational successes which reinforced the submariners' determination to get into the missile business, alarmed Fleet gunnery officers about their ability to defend against penetrations by cruise missiles and fended off Washington cost-cutters who wanted to emasculate REGULUS in the name of balancing the budget or substitute MATADOR as a cheaper missile. Examples are a 400 yard miss on Begg Rock by a CUSK to CARBONERO hand-off in September, 1948 and a LOON penetration of the First Fleet's air defense in November, 1948.

Many of the LOON technical successes are traceable to the "German Scientists" who migrated to Point Mugu. These included Willy Fiedler, Robert Lusser and Otto Schwede. But Dr. Herbert A. Wagner, now deceased, deserves special mention.

One day a young Marine pilot, well known as "Dirty" Dalby, came into my office and complained mildly about the lack of projects of potential benefit to the Marines. I knew he was flying F6Fs as a LOON simulator for Herbert Wagner who was then developing the command control computer. The next day I sat down with both of them and asked if the LOON system could be modified to yield an all-weather fighter close-air support system. In his methodical way Herbert ticked off the technical problems while Dirty chafed with eagerness to get started. Finally Herbert reached a can-do point and we worked up an in-house project to get it started.

In a few weeks they were getting 30 yard CEPs on a buoy off shore. As I recall, the system used an SCR-584 radar for tracking the F6F, a Reeves Plotting Board and command computer and the aircraft's regular voice radio and ordnance. The Marines got justifiably excited about this and soon arranged a contract out of Washington to General Electric for a militarized system named APQ-42 (?). Meantime the Korean War came along and Dirty Dalby's team with the prototype system went overseas and acquitted themselves nobly. Today, all-weather close-air support systems are a critical element in front-line combat.

This seems to be a good time to examine the notion that test facilities should be denied the opportunity to develop weapon hardware on the grounds that it interferes with their primary mission and competes with the defense industry. I have always felt that innovation will rise up in the ranks of engineers wherever they are found and that it is too valuable a commodity to be prohibited. The innovations which evolved from the LOON program and the development of SIDEWINDER at NOTS Inyokern bear this out. Dr. Royal Weller, longtime Chief Scientist at NAMTC, and Ralph Peterson are to be commended for their championing of innovation over the years.

So much for the boyhood of Point Mugu. I left in 1949 but nevertheless watched with pride as the range expanded in support of such missiles as LARK, SPARROW, REGULUS, RIGEL, POLARIS and TOMAHAWK. Looking forward, the range will surely be an essential facility in the current revitalization of the Navy and I'm sure this audience joins me in the hope that it will not be too busy making history to take the time to record it.

Grayson Merrill,
10264 Meadowview Dr.,
San Diego, CA 92131.

Index To

Reminiscences of

Captain Grayson Merrill

U.S. Navy (Retired)

Anderson, Robert B.
　As Secretary of the Treasury in the late 1950s, received an advance copy of the financial requirements of the Polaris missile development program, 179

Antiair Warfare
　Antiaircraft gunnery practice before World War II demonstrated the vulnerability of U.S. warships to air attack, 86, 158-159; use of target drones before and during World War II, 129, 158-160

Arkansas, USS (BB-33)
　Used for a 1931 training cruise to Europe for Naval Academy midshipmen, 15-21

B-24 Liberator
　Bomber in which Lieutenant Joseph P. Kennedy, Jr., was killed in August 1944 while trying to make a bombing attack on German rocket sites in France, 105, 115-116

Barnaby, Commander Ralph S., USN
　Work at the Naval Aircraft Factory in World War II, 80-81, 85, 104-105

Bombs
　Technique for operating radio-controlled glide bombs during World War II, 86-89, 95, 104; the German V-1 flying bomb was fired in demonstrations for U.S. military personnel at the end of World War II, 97; construction of glide bombs, 102

Braun, Wernher von
　See von Braun, Wernher

Bremen, Germany
　Site of a visit by U.S. technical personnel while observing German rocket and missile technology in 1945, 97-98

Brooks, USS (DD-232)
　Involved in fleet maneuvers during a fleet war game in the mid-1930s, 36-37, 40-41

Broome, Jack
　Civilian whose land was acquired by the government for the building of the Naval Air Missile Test Center at Point Mugu, California, shortly after World War II, 147-150

Bureau of Aeronautics
　Ran the assault drone and glide bomb programs in World War II, 77, 79-86, 88-89, 91-94, 100-102; relationship with BuOrd in World War II and beyond, 81, 120, 141-142; developed the air-launched Gorgon missile in World War II, 89-90, 112, 139-140; developed the Gargoyle air-to-ground missile in World War II, 90, 95; the chief of the Bureau declined to approve Merrill's 1945 proposal for developing missiles for shipboard use, 98; development of guided missiles in the early post-World War II period, 107-108, 112; in 1945 BuAer developed the Little Joe surface-to-air missile to

combat Japanese kamikazes, 112; oversaw the work of the Special Weapons Tactical Test and Evaluation Unit (SWTTEU), which was operated at Traverse City, Michigan, in World War II, 114; outlook for the bureau's post-World War II role in missile development, 128, 144-145; adjustment to peacetime environment, 128; connection with target drones in World War II, 129; approved a development program in the late 1940s to use the SCR-584 tracking radar to aid in close air support for Marine ground troops, 135-137; work of the electronic division in Pennsylvania in the early 1950s, 164-166; wide-ranging role in naval aviation, 167-168

Bureau of Ordnance
Relationship with BuAer in World War II and beyond, 81, 120, 141-142; development work in World War II on air-to-surface infrared homing missiles, 120-121; development and testing done in the late 1940s by the Naval Ordnance Test Station, Inyokern, California, 140; role in developing surface-to-air missiles following World War II, 155-156

Bureau of Yards and Docks
Role in the development of the Naval Air Missile Test Center at Point Mugu, California, shortly after World War II, 146-147

See also Seabees

Bush, Dr. Vannever
As presidential science adviser in the late 1940s, visited the Naval Air Missile Test Center at Point Mugu, California, 151-152

Carberry, Commander Deane E., CEC, USN
Managed the construction of facilities at the Naval Air Missile Test Center at Point Mugu, California, in the late 1940s, 147

Christensen, Commander Ernest E., Jr., USN (USNA, 1934)
Involved in Navy guided missile work in the 1940s, 25, 114, 131, 134

Cusk, USS (SS-348)
Test-fired a Loon missile (based on the German V-1 buzz bomb) off Naval Air Missile Test Center at Point Mugu, California, in 1947, 126-128

Dalby, Captain Marion C., USMC
Involved in a development program at the Naval Air Missile Test Center at Point Mugu, California, in the late 1940s to use the SCR-584 tracking radar to aid in close air support for Marine ground troops, 135-137

Davis, Midshipman Eugene W., USN (USNA, 1934)
Dated Merrill's girlfriend shortly before their graduation from the Naval Academy in 1934, 24-25

Decker, Lieutenant Commander Benton W., USN (USNA, 1920)
    Commanded the destroyer Dorsey (DD-117) in the mid-1930s, 42, 44

Denny, Reginald
    Movie actor who got involved with radio-controlled drones in World War II, 129

Dorsey, USS (DD-117)
    Operations off the West Coast in 1936, 41-43; living conditions on board, 42; material condition, 44-45; communications, 45-46

Draper, Dr. Stark
    Was a brilliant faculty member at the Massachusetts Institute of Technology in the early 1940s, 74-75

Drones
    The Navy's Bureau of Aeronautics ran an assault drone program in World War II, 77, 79-86, 91-94, 100-102, 106; the program eventually produced only limited combat use for a variety of reasons, 93-94, 99-103, 112; possibility of using kits to convert obsolete aircraft to assault drones, 101, 106; Lieutenant Joseph P. Kennedy, Jr., was killed in August 1944 in a radio-controlled B-24 while trying to make a bombing attack on German rocket sites in France, 105, 115-116; dismantling of the assault drone program at the end of the war, 111; use of target drones before and during World War II, 129, 158-160

Evans, Lieutenant Commander Clifton, Jr., USN
    Did development work on electronic warfare in the 1940s, 106

Fahrney, Captain Delmar S., USN (USNA, 1920)
    Work in the Bureau of Aeronautics with radio-controlled drone airplanes in the late 1930s and early 1940s, 76, 79-85, 91-94, 102, 106; relationship with BuOrd in World War II, 81, 120, 141-142; work on glide bombs, 88-89, 106; vision for postwar development and testing of Navy guided missiles, 92, 108-110, 112; received an overseas assignment in 1943 to aid his chances for promotion, 96, 142-143; arranged for the Navy to buy some German V-1 buzz bombs at the end of World War II, 125-126; outlook for BuAer's post-World War II role in missile development, 128, 144-145; duty in the Bureau of Aeronautics following World War II, 128, 143-145; approved a development program in the late 1940s to use the SCR-584 tracking radar to aid in close air support for Marine ground troops, 135-137; administration building at Point Mugu named in his honor, 146-147

Fairchild Aviation
    Merrill's work as chief engineer of the guided missile division in the late 1950s, 185-186

Families of Servicemen
    Youthful mischief by Merrill's son in Johnsville, Pennsylvania, in the early 1950s, 163-164

Fielding, Lieutenant Commander Charles F., USN
Commanded the destroyer Brooks (DD-232) in the mid-1930s, 36-37, 40-41

Flight Training
As conducted in various phases at Pensacola, Florida, in 1936-37, 49-53

Gage, Ensign Kenneth L., USNR
Served as a flight instructor at Pensacola, Florida, in the mid-1930s, 51

Gargoyle
Air-to-ground guided missile developed by the Bureau of Aeronautics during World War II, 90, 95

Gay, Ensign George H., USNR
Was the only survivor of Torpedo Squadron Eight in the 1942 Battle of Midway, 58-59

Germany
Success with the HS-293 glide bomb in combat in World War II, 88, 95; German rocket scientists demonstrated V-2s to U.S. personnel at the end of World War II, 96-97, 125; visit to a rathskeller in Bremen as part of the Americans' trip to Germany, 97-98; German scientists came to the United States after World War II to aid in research and development programs, 122-124, 137-138

Glide Bombs (Glombs)
Technique for operating radio-controlled glide bombs during World War II, 86-89, 95, 104; German success with the HS-293 in combat in World War II, 88, 95; built in World War II by inexperienced contractor, 102

Gorgon
Air-launched guided missile developed by the Bureau of Aeronautics during World War II, 89-90, 112, 139-140

Guided Missiles
See Missiles

Gunnery-Naval
Practice conducted by the battleship West Virginia (BB-48) in the mid-1930s, 34-35

Hatcher, Captain Robert S., USN (USNA, 1924)
Commanded the Naval Air Missile Test Center at Point Mugu, California, in the late 1940s, 123, 150

Hauck, Commander Hamilton O., USN (USNA, 1938)
Did work on electronic reliability in the late 1940s at Point Mugu, 106; proficiency flying, 157-158; post-Navy career in private industry, 185

Holloman, Major George V., USA
Army Air Forces officer who did development work in World War II, 81, 125

Holmes, Captain Melanie, USNR
Began her naval service as an enlisted yeoman in the Bureau of Aeronautics in World War II, 77-78, 115

Horney, Lieutenant (j.g.) Harry R., USN (USNA, 1927)
Served as a floatplane pilot in the mid-1930s, 39

Intelligence
Not much was available in the late 1930s to Torpedo Squadron Three concerning the Japanese Navy, 68-69

Jones, Lieutenant Robert F., USN (USNA, 1931)
Work with radio-controlled drone aircraft in the late 1930s and early 1940s, 81-84, 92-93, 100-102, 104, 109-110, 112, 159

Jupiter Missile
Army missile that was not used for the Polaris program because of its liquid fuel, 169-171, 173-175

Kamikazes
In 1945 the Bureau of Aeronautics developed the Little Joe surface-to-air missile to combat Japanese kamikazes, 112

Karman, Theodor von
See von Karman, Theodor

Kennedy, Lieutenant Joseph P., Jr, USNR
Killed in August 1944 in a B-24 while trying to make a bombing attack on German rocket sites in France, 105, 115-116

King, Admiral Ernest J., USN (USNA, 1901)
As Commander in Chief U.S. Fleet in World War II, was interested in BuAer's assault drone program, 82-84, 91-92, 94, 102

Lark
Early surface-to-air missile developed by the Bureau of Aeronautics in the 1940s, 107-108, 111, 155, 157

Leave and Liberty
Naval Academy midshipmen visited the Azores, Madeira, and Morocco during a summer training cruise in 1931, 20; leave trip to California by midshipmen in the summer of 1932, 21-23; while on destroyer duty in the mid-1930s, Merrill courted his future wife, 46-48

Lennox, Midshipman William R., USN (USNA, 1934)
   Involved in mischief while at the Naval Academy in the early 1930s, 16-17

Lewis, Midshipman Hugh H., USN (1934)
   Was involved in mischief during a Naval Academy training cruise in the summer of 1931, 15-16

Ley, Willie
   Former German rocket scientist who was involved in tests of the Loon (former German V-1 buzz bomb) at Naval Air Missile Test Center at Point Mugu, California, in the late 1940s, later in Polaris program, 138

Leydon, Commander John K., USN (USNA, 1938)
   Served as a strong advocate for the Naval Air Missile Test Center at Point Mugu, California, 128, 147, 149

Little Joe
   In 1945 the Bureau of Aeronautics developed this surface-to-air missile to combat Japanese kamikazes, 112, 119

Lockheed
   Defense contractor that had an important role in the development of the Polaris missile system in the late 1950s, 182

Loon
   U.S. Navy version of the German V-1 flying bomb, tested by the Naval Air Missile Test Center at Point Mugu, California, following World War II, 92, 125-128, 131, 138, 145-146, 150-151

Madeira
   The battleship <u>Arkansas</u> (BB-33) visited Funchal during the course of a 1931 training cruise, 15-16, 20

Magruder, Midshipman Peyton M., USN
   Was involved in mischief during a Naval Academy training cruise in the summer of 1931, 15-16

Marcoux, Midshipman Heliodore Aimé, USN (USNA, 1934)
   Involved in mischief while at the Naval Academy in the early 1930s, 16-17

Marine Corps, U.S.
   Development program at the Naval Air Missile Test Center at Point Mugu, California, in the late 1940s to use the SCR-584 tracking radar to aid in close air support for Marine ground troops, 135-137

Massachusetts Institute of Technology, Cambridge, Massachusetts
   Did early work on radar and computers in the 1940s, 71; Professor Stark Draper was an important faculty member, 74-75

Merrill, Captain Grayson, USN (Ret.) (USNA, 1934)
   Parents of, 1-5, 31, 33; boyhood in California in the 1910s and 1920s, 1-7; education of, 1-3, 13; Navy enlisted service, including boot camp and Naval Academy prep school, 1929-30, 5-6, 8-11; as a midshipman from 1930 to 1934 at the Naval Academy, 12-28; service in 1934-35 in the battleship West Virginia (BB-48), 28-40; married from 1936 to 1977 to the former Mary Elizabeth Wilson, 31-32, 40-41, 46-48, 53, 64, 73-74, 184, 186; service in 1935 in the destroyer Brooks (DD-232), 36-37, 40-41; service in 1936 in the destroyer Dorsey (DD-117), 41-48; flight training in 1936-37 at Pensacola, Florida, 49-53; service in Torpedo Squadron Three in the aircraft carrier Saratoga (CV-3) in the late 1930s, 54-70; took a course in electrical engineering at the Postgraduate School in the early 1940s, 70-75; children of, 73-74, 163-164, 186-188; service in the Bureau of Aeronautics from 1942 to 1945, 76-130; recommendations for post-World War II guided missile development and testing, 92, 98, 113-114; served as director of tests the Naval Air Missile Test Center at Point Mugu, California, in the late 1940s, 131-161; served in the Bureau of Aeronautics in the early 1950s, 161-162; duty in the 1950s at the electronics lab in Johnsville, Pennsylvania, 162-168; duty in 1956-57 as first technical director of the Polaris program, 169-184; authorship of books on guided missiles, 184-185; post-Navy civilian employment, 185-186; marriage to Jane Anthonsen in 1978, 187-188

Midway, Battle of
   Loss of TBD Devastators from Torpedo Squadron Eight in June 1942, 58-59

Missiles
   The Bureau of Aeronautics developed the Gorgon air-launched guided missile in World War II, 89-90, 112, 139-140; BuAer developed the air-to-ground Gargoyle missile in World War II, 90, 95; Lark was an early surface-to-air missile developed by the Bureau of Aeronautics in the 1940s, 107-108, 111, 155, 157; Regulus surface-to-surface missiles were important in the Cold War period, 108-109, 153; in 1945 the Bureau of Aeronautics developed the Little Joe surface-to-air missile to combat Japanese kamikazes, 112; Bureau of Ordnance development work in World War II on air-to-surface infrared homing missiles, 120; Point Mugu tested Loon missiles (based on German V-1 buzz bombs) in the late 1940s, 92, 125-128, 131, 138, 145-146, 150-151; outlook for BuAer's post-World War II role in missile development, 128; development and testing done in the late 1940s by the Naval Ordnance Test Station, Inyokern, California, 140; development of the Polaris submarine-launched ballistic missile in the late 1950s, 169-184; Fairchild Aviation's work on Army missile development in the late 1950s, 185-186

Mojave (California) Naval Air Station
   Served as a base of operations while the Naval Air Missile Test Center at Point Mugu, California, was being established in 1946, 131-133

Naval Academy, Annapolis, Maryland
Prospective midshipmen got ready for entrance exams in 1930 by attending a Navy-run prep school at San Diego, 9-11; academics in the early 1930s, 13, 24; mischief on the part of midshipmen, 13-17; summer training cruise on board the battleship <u>Arkansas</u> (BB-33) in 1931, 17-21; disciplinary infractions, 24-25; the entire class of 1934 graduated, though not all of the preceding class had, 26, 28; bonding of midshipmen as classmates, 26-27

Naval Aircraft Factory, Philadelphia, Pennsylvania
Role in drone development programs during World War II, 79-85, 100, 103-104; development of the Little Joe missile at the end of World War II, 112; in 1945 produced the Little Joe surface-to-air missile to combat Japanese kamikazes, 112

Naval Air Missile Test Center, Point Mugu, California
Merrill's role in proposing and selecting Point Mugu as the site for post-World War II Navy guided missile testing, 92, 113-114; testing of the Lark surface-to-air missile in 1950, 111, 157; commissioned in October 1946, 114; received the services of former German rocket scientists in the late 1940s, 122-124; tested Loon missiles (based on German V-1 buzz bombs) in the late 1940s, 126-128, 145-146, 150-151; came into being in 1946 with assistance out of the naval air station at Mojave, California, 131-134; development program to use the SCR-584 tracking radar to aid in close air support for Marine ground troops, 135-137; work of U.S. rocket expert Robert Truax, 139-140; construction of the physical facilities in the late 1940s, 146; acquisition of land for the station, 147-150; visit by Dr. Vannever Bush, President Truman's science adviser, 151-152; testing of the Regulus missile, 153; relationship with defense contractors, 157

Naval Ordnance Test Station, Inyokern, California
Role as a development and test site for BuOrd in World War II and afterward, 120-121, 140, 142; overhauled phototheodolites in World War II for the Special Weapons Tactical Test and Evaluation Unit, 121

Naval Postgraduate School, Annapolis, Maryland
Course in electrical engineering at the beginning of the 1940s, 70-75

Naval Research Laboratory, Anacostia, D.C.
Role in drone development programs during World War II, 100; had temporary control of German rocket scientists brought to the United States after the war, 122-123

Naval Reserve, U.S.
Provided important manpower to supplement the regular Navy during World War II, 118

Nimitz, Fleet Admiral Chester W., USN (USNA, 1905)
As Chief of Naval Operations, visited the Naval Air Missile Test Center at Point Mugu, California, for test firing of the Loon missile in 1947, 126-128

Norton Sound, USS (AVM-1)
Former seaplane tender used for missile testing off the West Coast in the late 1940s, 154

Nuclear Weapons
The atomic bombs dropped on Japan in 1945 paved the way for post-World War II weapons development, 99

Pearl Harbor, Hawaii
Mock attack in 1937 by planes from the aircraft carrier Saratoga (CV-3), 64-65

Pehrson, Gordon O.
Initiated the Program Evaluation Review Technique (PERT) to track progress in the Polaris program in the late 1950s, 172-173, 176-179, 182-183

Perkins, Captain Albert N., USN (USNA, 1924)
Served as the first commanding officer when the Naval Air Missile Test Center at Point Mugu, California, was commissioned in 1946, 133-134

PERT
See Program Evaluation Review Technique (PERT)

Point Mugu, California
See Naval Air Missile Test Center

Polaris Program
Kicked off with recommendation by Dr. Edward Teller in the mid-1950s, 99, early gathering of the staff in 1956, 169-171; decision not to use the liquid-fueled Jupiter, 169-171, 173-175; use of the Program Evaluation Review Technique (PERT) to monitor progress in the program in the late 1950s, 172-173, 176-178, 182-183; Navy relationship with the defense contractors involved in the program, 181-182

Program Evaluation Review Technique (PERT)
Used to monitor progress in the Polaris program in the late 1950s, 172-173, 176-178, 182-183

Raborn, Rear Admiral William F., Jr., USN (USNA, 1928)
Ran the Polaris submarine-launched ballistic missile program in the late 1950s, 95, 156, 162, 168-184; style of management and leadership, 172, 175-176, 178-180

Radar
Development program at the Naval Air Missile Test Center at Point Mugu, California, in the late 1940s to use the SCR-584 tracking radar to aid in close air support for Marine ground troops, 135-137

Radio
 Used for communication by planes of Torpedo Squadron Three in the late 1930s, 53-54, 56, 61; at the naval communications facility in Annapolis, Maryland, in the early 1940s, 72; use in controlling drone aircraft in World War II, 85-86, 129

 See also Drones

Recruit Training
 At San Diego in 1929, 8-9

Regulus
 Surface-to-surface missile that was important in the Cold War period, 108-109, 153

Root, L. Eugene
 Lockheed vice president who was involved in the Polaris missile development in the late 1950s, 182

Saratoga, USS (CV-3)
 Operations of Torpedo Squadron Three in the late 1930s, 54-70; mock attack on Pearl Harbor in 1937, 64-65

SATFOR
 See Special Air Task Force

Scoles, Captain Albert B., USN (USNA, 1927)
 Commanded the Pilotless Aircraft Unit in 1945-46 as the Naval Air Missile Test Center was being established at Point Mugu, California, 133-134

Seabees
 Established a base at Point Mugu, California, in World War II, 114, 131-133; role in building up the Naval Air Missile Test Center at Point Mugu after the war, 147-148

Shafroth, Commander John F., Jr., USN (USNA, 1908)
 Served as executive officer of the battleship West Virginia (BB-48) in the mid-1930s, 33

Sharp, Lieutenant Sidney A., USN
 Served as a liaison officer with German rocket scientists who worked at the Naval Air Missile Test Center at Point Mugu, California, in the late 1940s, 123-124, 135

Smith, Captain Levering, USN (USNA, 1932)
 Joined the staff of the Polaris program in 1956 because of his knowledge of solid propellants, later became technical director, 171, 173, 175-176, 178

Smith, Captain Oscar, USN (USNA, 1908)
 Had an important role in the Navy's assault drone program in World War II, 82-83, 91-94, 115

Smith, Midshipman Roy C. III, USN
    Was kicked out of the Naval Academy in 1933 when apprehended coming back from unauthorized absence, 14-15

Special Air Task Force (SATFOR)
    Work with U.S. Navy assault drones in World War II, 82, 92, 99-100, 103, 112; dismantled at the end of the war, 114

Special Weapons Tactical Test and Evaluation Unit (SWTTEU)
    Operated at Traverse City, Michigan, in World War II, 114, 121, 129, 131, 133, 159

Stone, Ensign Lester J. Stone, USN (USNA, 1934)
    Went through flight training at Pensacola in the mid-1930s, 49; survived a crash in a TBD Devastator, 55, 62

SWTTEU
    <u>See</u> Special Weapons Tactical Test and Evaluation Unit (SWTTEU)

TBD Devastator
    Flown by Torpedo Squadron Three from the aircraft carrier <u>Saratoga</u> (CV-3) in the late 1930s, 55-56; tactics for torpedo delivery, 58-59; losses in the 1942 Battle of Midway, 58-59

TG Torpedo Plane
    Flown by Torpedo Squadron Three in the late 1930s, 54-57

Tactics
    For delivery of torpedoes by the TBD Devastator in the late 1930s, 58-59

Teller, Dr. Edward
    His recommendation in the mid-1950s kicked off the program for a submarine-launched ballistic missile, 99; role in shifting to a smaller-than-planned warhead, 173-175

Torpedo Squadron Three (VT-3)
    Operated from the aircraft carrier <u>Saratoga</u> (CV-3) in the late 1930s, 54-70; tactics for torpedo delivery, 58-59; mock attack on Pearl Harbor in 1937, 64-65

Towers, Vice Admiral John H., USN (USNA, 1906)
    Opposed the combat deployment of assault drone aircraft in World War II, 94, 102-103

Training
    Recruit training at San Diego in 1929, 8-9; midshipman summer training cruise on board the battleship <u>Arkansas</u> (BB-33) in 1931, 17-21; flight training was conducted in various phases at Pensacola, Florida, in 1936-37, 49-53

Truax, Lieutenant Robert C., USN (USNA, 1939)
Work in World War II and afterward on various rocket systems, 92, 114, 133, 139-140

Truman, President Harry S
Approved the concept to establish the Naval Air Missile Test Center at Point Mugu, California, shortly after World War II, 130, 146

Tucker, Captain Dundas P., USN (USNA, 1925)
While assigned to the Bureau of Ordnance in World War II, had an excellent relationship with Del Fahrney of the Bureau of Aeronautics, 81, 120, 141

Tuttle, Ensign Melbourne W., USNR
Reserve officer who got involved with radio-controlled drones in World War II, 129, 159

Tuve, Merle
Individual who had an instrumental role in the World War II development of the proximity fuze for antiaircraft projectiles, 119-120

Utility Squadron Three (VJ-3)
Flew target drones for antiaircraft practice prior to World War II, 159

Utility Squadron Five (VJ-5)
Developed and tested radio-controlled assault drones during World War II, 83-84, 91, 100, 104

V-1
German flying bomb fired in demonstrations for U.S. military personnel at the end of World War II, 97; supplies taken to the United States after the war, 125-126

See also Loon

V-2
German rocket fired in demonstrations for U.S. military personnel at the end of World War II, 96-97

VJ-3
See Utility Squadron Five

VJ-5
See Utility Squadron Three

VT-3
See Torpedo Squadron Three

Vieweg, Captain Walter V. R., USN (1924)
Headed a board that in 1945 surveyed sites for a postwar missile-testing range, 113; member of the "gun club," 156

von Braun, Wernher
German rocket scientist who came to the United States at the end of World War II and worked on projects for the U.S. Army, 122, 170, 181

von Karman, Theodor
CalTech rocket scientist who accompanied U.S. military personnel for rocket demonstrations in Germany at the end of World War II, 96-98, 125; suggested use of rockets from warships, 98

Wagner, Dr. Herbert
Austrian who did development work on the German HS-293 glide bomb during World War II, 88; came to the United States after World War II to aid U.S. Navy development programs, 122-124, 136, 181

Watson, Clement H.
Work on the Polaris development program in the late 1950s, 177-179

West Virginia, USS (BB-48)
Operations off the West Coast in the mid-1930s, 28-40; gunnery practice, 34-35; operated floatplanes for spotting gunfire, 39

Wilkins, Sir Hubert
British Arctic explorer who made an unsuccessful attempt to reach the North Pole by submarine in 1931, 18

Women
Enlisted yeoman provided excellent service in the Bureau of Aeronautics in World War II, 77-78

Wyoming, USS (BB-32)
Had to tow the research submarine Nautilus to Ireland after it broke down in June 1931, 18

www.ingramcontent.com/pod-product-compliance
Lightning Source LLC
Chambersburg PA
CBHW080613170426
43209CB00007B/1423